RÉNYI PICTURE DICTIONARY

FRENCH AND ENGLISH

ÉDITIONS RÉNYI INC.

355 Adelaide Street West, Suite 400, Toronto, Ontario Canada M5V 1S2

The Rényi French Picture Dictionary

Copyright © 1990 Éditions Rényi Inc.

Illustrated by Kathryn Adams, Pat Gangnon, Colin Gillies, David Shaw and Yvonne Zan.
Cover illustration by Colin Gillies. Designed by David Shaw and Associates.

Color separations by New Concept Limited

Printed in Singapore by Khai Wah Litho Pte Limited

Edited by Sophie Arthaud, René Le Bel, Gina Lepage, Pierre Rényi, Patrice Soulard

The Rényi French Picture Dictionary   ISBN 0-921606-47-8

INTRODUCTION

Some of Canada's best illustrators have contributed to this dictionary, which has been carefully designed to appeal to children, so that learning new words can be a pleasure.

Its unusually large number of terms – 3336 – makes the dictionary a flexible teaching tool. Because the vocabulary it encompasses is so broad, this dictionary can also be used to teach English as a Second Language to older children and adults, as well as helping young children acquire language skills.

NOTE TO TEACHERS AND PARENTS

In a children's dictionary, the most difficult decision is usually which words to include and which ones to leave out. Here, word selection has been based partly on word frequency analysis of English usage (in order to include the most commonly used terms), and partly on thematic clustering (in order to cover major fields of activity or interest).

This process was further complicated by the decision to systematically illustrate the meanings. Although the degree of abstraction has been kept reasonably low, it was deemed necessary to include terms such as "to expect" and "to forgive", which are virtually impossible to illustrate, given the space and other constraints. Instead of dropping these words, we decided to provide explanatory sentences that create a context.

Where variations occur between British and North-American English, both terms are given with an asterisk marking the British version (favor/favour*, gas/petrol*). Both variants are listed alphabetically in the index.

The alphabetical index at the end of the book lists every term in the dictionary with the number of its corresponding illustration. Teachers could use this feature to expand children's numeracy skills, by asking the child to match an index number with the actual illustration, as well as using it to train students in dictionary skills.

Great care has been taken to ensure that any contextual statements made are factual, have some educational value and are compatible with statements made elsewhere in the book. Lastly, from a strictly psychological viewpoint, the little girl featured in the book has not been made into a paragon of virtue; children will readily identify with her imperfections.

À TOUS MES NOUVEAUX AMIS

Je m'appelle Julie. Je vais à l'école. J'apprends à nager. J'ai un petit frère et mille idées. Si tu veux rencontrer mon papa, qui est amiral, regarde à droite au bas de la page. Maman est à la page suivante, en haut. Pour faire ma connaissance, rends-toi directement au mot ''calme''.

Les gens pensent parfois que les dictionnaires sont des livres ennuyeux. C'est sans doute qu'ils n'ont jamais vu celui-ci, qui parle de moi, de ma famille et de mes amis.

Cinq grandes personnes se sont beaucoup amusées à faire les illustrations. Moi, j'ai dessiné une image, celle du zèbre : essaie de la trouver!

Je dois te quitter maintenant. Mais tu me retrouveras, page après page.

julie

le boulier

1   abacus

de, environ, autour de

Parle-moi **de** cela.
Cela prend **environ**
une heure.
Jacques regarde
autour de lui.

Tell me about it.
It takes about an hour.
Jacques looks about him.

2   about

La pomme est **au-dessus**
de sa tête.

3   above

Paul est **absent** aujourd'hui.

4   absent

Toutes les autos ont
un accélérateur.

5   accelerator

un accent

John a **un accent**
britannique.
Mets **l'accent** sur la
première syllabe.

John has a British accent.
Put the accent on the first
syllable.

6   accent

un accident

7   accident

un accordéon

8   accordion

On **a accusé** Sophie.

9   to accuse

un as de pique

10   ace

J'ai mal à la tête.

11   My head **aches**.

Un acide peut brûler la peau.

12   acid

Le gland est le fruit du chêne.

13   acorn

une acrobate

14   acrobat

de l'autre côté, à travers

Paul habite **de l'autre côté**
de la rue.
Alice court **à travers**
champs.

Paul lives across the street.
Alice runs across the fields.

15   across

additionner

2 + 2 =

16   to add

C'est **l'adresse** de Julie.

17   address

Le papa de Julie est **amiral**.

18   admiral

Bertrand **adore** Claire.

19   to adore

Un adulte est une grande personne.

20   adult

Avance ton roi!

21   to advance

Barnabé a **l'avantage**.

22   advantage

La maman de Julie aime **l'aventure**.

23   adventure

Philippe **a peur**.

24   He is **afraid**.

L'Afrique est un continent.

25   Africa

après

Tu peux jouer **après** le dîner.
Répète **après** moi!
Cours **après** la balle!

You can play after dinner.
Repeat after me!
Run after the ball!

26   after

L'après-midi commence à 12 heures.

27   afternoon

encore, de nouveau

Joue **encore** ce morceau!
C'est ton tour **de nouveau**.

Play it again!
It is your turn again.

28   again

Minou se frotte **contre** les jambes de François.

29   to rub **against**

Quelle différence d'**âge**!

30   age

une personne **agile**

31   **agile** person

Le bateau **s'est échoué**.

32   aground

devant, à l'avance

Hélène est assise **devant** Pierre.
Planifie tes vacances **à l'avance**!

Hélène sits ahead of Pierre.
Plan ahead for your holidays!

33   ahead

porter **secours**

34   to provide **aid**

Est-ce qu'elle **vise** bien la cible?

35   to aim

Le cerf-volant plane dans **l'air**.

36   air

Zénon dort sur **le matelas pneumatique**.

37   air mattress

un insecte dans un vase **hermétique**

38   airtight

Cet **avion** semble en difficulté.

39   airplane/aeroplane*

Les avions atterrissent à l'**aéroport**.

40   airport

une allée, un couloir

41   aisle

le **réveil**, le **réveille-matin**

42   alarm clock

un album de photos

43   album

La maison est **en feu**.

44   alight

L'un des deux poissons est bien **vivant**.

45   alive

Je les veux **tous**.

46   I want them **all**.

un chat dans la ruelle

47   alley

un alligator

48   alligator

une amande

49   almond

Milou peut **presque** attraper l'os.

50   almost

Pourquoi est-il **seul**?

51   alone

Nous marchons **le long de** la rivière.

52   along

à haute voix

53   aloud

un alphabet

A B C D E F G H I J K L M
N O P Q R S T U V W X Y Z

a b c d e f g h i j k l m
n o p q r s t u v w x y z

54   alphabet

Est-ce que je dois **déjà** partir?

55   Do I have to go **already**?

Je n'ai **pas de mal**, ça va.

56   I am **alright**.

J'en veux **aussi**.

57   I **also** want some.

une échelle en **aluminium**

58   aluminum/aluminium* ladder

Je tombe **toujours**.

59   I **always** fall down.

ambulance

une ambulance

60   ambulance

un loup **parmi** les moutons

61   wolf **among** sheep

une ancre

62   anchor

des ruines **anciennes**

63   ancient

un angle

64   angle

Il est **fâché**.

65   He is **angry**.

les animaux

66   animals

la cheville

67   ankle

annoncer

68   to **announce**

un **autre** sandwich

69   **another** sandwich

La réponse est...

70   The **answer** is...

la fourmi

71   ant

L'Antarctique

72   Antarctic

une antilope

73   antelope

les bois de l'élan

74   antlers

Je **n'ai pas** d'argent.

75 I do not have **any** money.

Ça mange **de tout**.

76   It eats **anything**.

Il ne peut aller **nulle part**.

77 He cannot go **anywhere**.

à part, séparé

78   apart

le singe

79   ape

la ruche des abeilles

80   apiary

---

faire ses excuses, excuser

Faire ses excuses, c'est demander pardon.
Excusez-moi d'être en retard!

To apologize means to say you are sorry.
I apologize for being late!

81   to apologize/apologise*

---

apparaître

Le magicien a fait **apparaître** un lapin.
Le soleil **apparaît** à l'horizon.

The magician made a rabbit appear.
The sun appears on the horizon.

82   to appear

---

applaudir

83   to applaud

---

la pomme

84   apple

---

le trognon de pomme

85   apple core

---

approcher

86   to approach

---

un abricot

87   apricot

En **avril**, ne te découvre pas d'un fil!

88   April

---

le tablier

89   apron

---

un aquarium

90   aquarium

---

une arche

91   arch

---

un architecte

92   architect

Il fait un froid glacial dans **l'Arctique**.

93   Arctic

---

discuter, se disputer

94   to argue

---

le bras

95   arm

---

le fauteuil

96   armchair

Le chevalier porte **une armure**.

97   armor/armour*

---

une aisselle

98   armpit

---

autour, environ, vers

Autour du monde en quatre-vingts jours
Un autobus pèse **environ** 6 tonnes.
Nous y serons **vers** midi.

Around the world in eighty days
A bus weighs around 6 tons.
We will be there around noon.

99   around

arranger des fleurs	Le policier **arrête** Jules.	**arriver**	la **flèche**
100 to **arrange** flowers	101 to **arrest**	102 to **arrive**	103 arrow

un **artichaut**	un **artiste**	**aussi, comme** Toto est **aussi** grand que Patrice. Le petit frère de Paul est beau **comme** un coeur! *Toto is as tall as Patrice.* *Paul's little brother is really cute!*	la **cendre**
104 artichoke	105 artist	106 as	107 ash

le **cendrier**	**L'Asie** est un continent.	**demander** son chemin	Marie et son chat sont tous deux **endormis**.
108 ashtray	109 Asia	110 to **ask** for directions	111 asleep

les **asperges**	Il lui faudra peut-être deux **aspirines**.	Patrick **a étonné** Jeanne.	un **astronaute**
112 asparagus	113 aspirin	114 to **astonish**	115 astronaut

un **astronome**	**à, au** Hélène est **à** la maison avec son papa. Ils regardent le tableau. Va **au** lit tout de suite! *Hélène is at home with her father.* *They are looking at the picture.* *Go to bed at once!*	une **athlète**	un **atlas**
116 astronomer	117 at	118 athlete	119 atlas

l'atmosphère de la terre	**un atome**	**attacher**	Fais **attention**!
120 atmosphere	121 atom	122 to attach	123 Pay **attention**!
le grenier	**un auditoire**	**Août** est le huitième mois de l'année.	Ma **tante** est la sœur de ma mère.
124 attic	125 audience	126 August	127 My **aunt** is my mother's sister.
L'Australie est la plus grande île du monde.	**un auteur**	un réveil **automatique**	**L'automne** est l'une des quatre saisons.
128 Australia	129 author	130 automatic	131 autumn
une avalanche	**un avocat**	Pourquoi Jules reste-t-il **éveillé**?	Elle est **partie**.
132 avalanche	133 avocado	134 awake	135 She is **away**.
une **affreuse** odeur	une personne **maladroite**	**une hache**	**Un essieu** relie deux roues.
136 an **awful** smell	137 an **awkward** person	138 axe	139 axle

B

le bébé

140　　baby

la voiture d'enfant

141　baby carriage/pram*

Gratte-moi **le dos**!

142　　back

des œufs au **lard**

144　bacon and eggs

Cette pomme est **mauvaise**.

145　　bad apple

un insigne

146　　badge

reculer

143　　to back up

Qu'est-ce qu'il y a dans **le sac**?

147　　bag

un appât à souris

148　　bait

cuire, faire cuire

149　　to bake

Le boulanger cuit du pain.

150　　baker

la boulangerie

151　　bakery

L'acrobate est bien en **équilibre** sur la corde.

152　good balance

le balcon

153　　balcony

Pierrot est **chauve**.

154　　bald

la balle

155　　ball

la ballerine

156　　ballerina

le ballet

157　　ballet

le ballon

158　　balloon

la montgolfière

159   hot air **balloon**

la banane

160   banana

le bandeau

161   band

un orchestre

162   musical **band**

Le pansement fait du bien à Michel.

163   bandage

frapper

164   to bang

Michel descend l'escalier sur **la rampe**.

165   banister

Michel porte son argent à **la banque**.

166   bank

la barre

167   bar

Les bars sont réservés aux adultes.

168   bar/pub*

le fil de fer barbelé

169   barbed wire

Le coiffeur lui coupe les cheveux.

170   barber

un pied nu

171   one **bare** foot

une aubaine, des soldes

172   bargain

la péniche

173   barge

aboyer

174   to bark

L'orge pousse dans les champs.

176   barley

la grange

177   barn

la caserne des soldats

178   barracks

une écorce

175   bark

le tonneau, la barrique

179   barrel

le canon du revolver

180   barrel

la barrette

181   barrette/hair slide*

la barrière

182   barrier

la base de la colonne

183   base

le but de base-ball

184   base

le base-ball

185   baseball

le sous-sol

186   basement/cellar*

le basilic

187   basil

le panier

188   basket

le basket-ball

189   basketball

les bâtons

190   bats

Je prends **un bain**.

192   I am having a bath.

la salle de bains

193   bathroom

la baignoire

194   bathtub

La chauve-souris chasse la nuit.

191   bat

une pile électrique pour ta radio

195   battery

Le bateau navigue dans **la baie**.

196   bay

Maman épice le ragoût avec des feuilles de **laurier**.

197   bay leaves

le bazar

198   bazaar

être

Promets-moi d'**être** gentil!
Antoine **est** très intelligent.
Roméo et Juliette
sont amoureux.

*Promise me that you
will be good!'*
Antoine is very intelligent.
Romeo and Juliet are in love.

199   to be

la plage

200   beach

la perle

201   bead

le bec

202   beak

le faisceau de lumière

203   **beam** of light

les haricots, les fèves

204   beans

L'ours fait du vélo.

205   bear

Pépé a **une** longue **barbe**.

206   beard

Quelle horrible **bête**!

207   beast

Paulette **bat** le tambour.

208   to beat

Fifi est **belle**!

209   beautiful

le castor

210   beaver

Je pleure **parce que**...

211   I am crying **because**...

devenir

La chenille

devient

papillon.

212   to become

le lit

213   bed

ia lampe de chevet

214 bed lamp/reading light*

la chambre à coucher

215   bedroom

L'abeille est un insecte utile.

216   bee

un hêtre

217   beech

Les abeilles vivent
dans **la ruche.**

218   beehive

une chope de bière	**la betterave**	**le scarabée**	Lave-toi les mains **avant** le dîner!
219 beer	220 beet/beetroot*	221 beetle	222 Wash your hands **before** dinner.
mendier	**commencer** Pour **commencer**, prenons le petit déjeuner. La leçon de piano de Julie **commence** à dix heures. *To begin with, let's have breakfast. Julie's piano lesson begins at ten o'clock.*	Alice **se conduit bien**.	Noémie se cache **derrière** l'arbre.
223 to beg	224 to begin	225 to behave	226 behind
beige	Je **crois** aux dragons.	**la cloche, la clochette**	**le nombril**
227 beige	228 I **believe** in dragons.	229 bell	230 belly button
Il m'**appartient**.	Le chat est **en dessous** de la table.	**la ceinture**	**le banc**
231 He **belongs** to me.	232 below	233 belt	234 bench
le tournant de la route	**plier, tordre**	Marcel porte **un béret**.	Patricia est **à côté** de l'arbre.
235 bend	236 to bend	237 beret	238 beside

autre, d'ailleurs

Ne crois-tu pas que tu
devrais manger **autre** chose
que du dessert?
D'ailleurs, tu ne devrais pas
manger tant de sucre.

*Should you not eat
something else besides
dessert?
Besides, you should not eat
so much sugar.*

239   besides

la meilleure

240   best

mieux, meilleur

Julie écrit **mieux**
que David.
Les fruits sont **meilleurs**
que le chocolat.

*Julie writes better
than David.
Fruit is better than
chocolate.*

241   better

Philippe marche **entre**
les rochers.

242   between

le bavoir

243   bib

la bicyclette, le vélo

244   bicycle

grand

245   big

Le vélo de Philippe a
un guidon de course.

246   bike

le billet

247   bill/banknote*

le panneau d'affichage

248   billboard/hoarding*

le jeu de billard

249   billiards/snooker*

attacher

250   to bind/tie up*

les jumelles

251   binoculars

un oiseau

252   bird

la naissance

Julie pesait sept livres
à **la naissance**.
La chatte a donné **naissance**
à quatre petits chatons.

*Julie weighed seven pounds
at birth.
The cat gave birth to
four little kittens.*

253   birth

Bon **anniversaire**!

254   birthday

le biscuit

255   biscuit

Frédéric **mord** à belles
dents dans son sandwich.

256   to bite

la bouchée, la morsure

257   bite

amer

La bière a un goût **amer**.
Julie a versé des larmes
amères quand elle a perdu
sa poupée.

*Beer has a bitter taste.
Julie wept bitter tears when
she lost her doll.*

258   bitter

noir

259 black

la mûre

260 blackberry

le merle

261 blackbird

le tableau noir

262 blackboard

le cassis

263 blackcurrant

le forgeron

264 blacksmith

la lame de l'épée

265 blade

blâmer, reprocher

Papa a **reproché** à Julie d'avoir cassé le vase, mais elle est innocente.
C'est David que Papa devrait **blâmer**!

Father blamed Julie for breaking the vase, but she did not do it.
Father should blame David!

266 to blame

la page vierge

267 blank page

la couverture

268 blanket

Une explosion fait un bruit de tonnerre.

269 blast

faire sauter

270 to blast

le feu, l'incendie

271 blaze

le veston, le blazer

272 blazer

L'eau de javel sert à blanchir le linge.

273 bleach

Elle saigne du nez.

274 to bleed

le mélangeur

275 blender

un aveugle

276 blind

cligner des yeux

277 to blink

Une ampoule, ça fait mal!

278 blister

la tempête de neige

279   blizzard

le cube

280   block

le pâté de maisons

281   block

Le policier lui **bloque** le chemin.

282   to block

les cheveux **blonds**

283   blond/blonde*

une transfusion de **sang**

284   blood

la floraison

285   bloom

Au printemps, les arbres **fleurissent**.

286   to blossom

une grosse **tache** d'encre

287   blot

la blouse, le chemisier

288   blouse

un coup sur la tête

289   a **blow** to the head

souffler

290   to blow

bleu

291   blue

la myrtille, le bleuet

292   blueberries

émoussé

La lame du couteau est trop **émoussée** pour couper la tomate.
Alice n'a pas ménagé ses mots avec lui!

*The blade of the knife is too blunt to cut the tomato.
Alice was very blunt with him.*

293   blunt

Caroline **rougit** facilement.

294   to blush

le sanglier

295   boar

la planche

296   board

se vanter

Christophe **se vante** tout le temps.
Il ne peut pas **se vanter** d'être modeste!

*Christophe is always boasting.
His modesty is nothing to boast about!*

297   to boast

le canot, la barque

298   boat

une épingle à cheveux

299   bobby pin/hairgrip*

le corps humain

300   body

bouillir

301   to boil

le boulon

302   bolt

un os pour le chien

303   bone

le feu de joie

304   bonfire

le livre

305   book

une étagère à livres

306   bookshelf

le boomerang

307   boomerang

la botte

308   boot

la frontière entre deux pays

309   border

C'est dur de **percer** un trou dans du béton!

310   to bore

né

En quelle année es-tu **né**?
C'est un meneur-**né**.

What year were you born?
He is a born leader.

312   born

emprunter

Julie **emprunte** souvent
la bicyclette de son frère.

Julie often borrows her
brother's bike.

313   to borrow

le patron

314   boss

ennuyer

Julie **ennuie** parfois
les gens à en mourir!
Robert m'**ennuie** avec
toutes ses paroles.

Julie can bore people
to death!
Robert bores me because
he talks too much.

311   to bore

tous deux

Natalie et Mathieu sont
tous deux mignons.
Tous deux ont un gentil
sourire.

Natalie and Mathieu are
both cute.
Both have a nice smile.

315   both

la bouteille

316   bottle

un ouvre-bouteille, un décapsuleur

317   bottle opener

le fond de l'aquarium

318   bottom

un gros caillou 319 boulder	**Le ballon rebondit.** 320 to **bounce**	**un bouquet** de fleurs 321 bouquet	**un arc** et des flèches 322 bow
le bol 324 bowl	Y a-t-il quelque chose dans **la boîte?** 325 box	**le boxeur** 326 boxer	**le nœud papillon** 323 bow tie
le garçon 327 boy	**le soutien-gorge** 328 bra	**le bracelet** 329 bracelet	**se vanter** Noémie **se vante** d'avoir beaucoup de jouets. Son papa lui dit de ne pas **se vanter**. *Noémie brags about the number of toys she has. Her father tells her not to brag.* 330 to **brag**
le cerveau 331 brain	Pour arrêter la voiture, on utilise **les freins**. 332 brake	**freiner** 333 to **brake**	**la branche** de l'arbre 334 branch
courageux Le dentiste dit que tu as été très **courageuse**, Julie. *The dentist says you were very brave, Julie.* 335 brave	**le pain** 336 bread	La lampe **est cassée**. 337 to **break**	La voiture est **en panne**. 338 to **break down**

Le voleur **est** entré par effraction.	le petit déjeuner	Le dragon a mauvaise **haleine**.	respirer
339 to **break** in	340 breakfast	341 breath	342 to breathe

la brique	Le maçon construit un mur de briques.	La mariée est un peu timide.	Le marié aussi.
343 brick	344 bricklayer	345 bride	346 bridegroom

le pont	la bride du cheval	la serviette	un soleil éclatant
347 bridge	348 bridle	349 briefcase	350 bright sun

Milou **apporte** les pantoufles.	Julie **rapporte** les livres à la bibliothèque.	un verre **cassant**	le brocoli
351 to bring	352 to bring back	353 brittle glass	354 broccoli

la broche	Le ruisseau court à travers champs.	le balai	J'aime mon **frère**.
355 brooch	356 brook	357 broom	358 I love my **brother**.

le sourcil

359   brow

brun

360   brown

Martin a besoin de se **brosser** les cheveux.

362   to brush

la brosse

363   brush

Mathieu a **un bleu** au bras.

361   bruise

des choux de Bruxelles

366   brussels sprouts

le pinceau

364   paintbrush

la brosse à dents

365   toothbrush

Brigitte aime les bains pleins de **bulles**.

367   bubble

le seau

368   bucket

la boucle d'une ceinture

369   belt buckle

le bourgeon

370   bud

le bison

371   buffalo

un insecte

372   bug

le clairon du soldat

373   bugle

construire

374   to build

le taureau

375   bull

le bulldozer

376   bulldozer

Les balles de fusil sont dangereuses.

377   bullet

le porte-voix

378 bullhorn/megaphone*

Cet homme est **une brute**.

379　　bully

Laurent a **une bosse** sur la tête.

380　　bump

les pare-chocs

381　　bumpers

la botte d'asperges

382　　bunch

le fagot de bois

383　　bundle

la bouée

384　　buoy

le cambrioleur

385　　burglar

Le feu **brûle** dans l'âtre.

386　　to burn

Boum! Le ballon **éclate**.

387　　to burst

enterrer

388　　to bury

un autobus

389　　bus

un arrêt d'autobus

390　　bus stop

Un arbuste est plus petit qu'un　　arbre.

391　　bush

Pas maintenant, je suis **occupé**.

392　　I am **busy** now.

mais

Je voudrais bien venir, **mais** je suis occupé.
Paul est grand, **mais** sa soeur est plus grande encore.

I would like to come, but I am busy.
Paul is big, but his sister is bigger.

393　　but

le boucher

394　　butcher

le beurre

395　　butter

le papillon

396　　butterfly

les boutons

397　　buttons

Philippe **achète** une crème glacée.

398　　to buy

le chou

399   cabbage

la cabane dans la forêt

400   cabin

une armoire

401   cabinet

le câble

402   cable/lead*

le cactus

403   cactus

la cage

404   cage

le gâteau

405   cake

la calculatrice

406   calculator

le calendrier

407   calendar

Le veau est le petit de la vache.

408   calf

appeler

409   to call

Julie est toujours **calme**.

412   She is **calm**.

le chameau

413   camel

un appareil-photo

414   camera

annuler

Nous annulerons le pique-nique s'il pleut.
Julie **a annulé** notre visite au zoo.

We will call off the picnic if it rains.
Julie has called off our trip to the zoo.

410   to **call off**

Lucie et France **campent** sous la tente.

415   to camp

le campement

416   campsite

la boîte

417   can

téléphoner

411   to **call up**/to **phone***

un ouvre-boîte

418 can opener/tin* opener

Le bateau vogue sur **le canal**.

419   canal

le canari

420   canary

la bougie

421   candle

le chandelier

422   candlestick

les bonbons

423   candy/sweets*

Il marche avec **une canne**.

424   cane/walking stick*

le canon

425   cannon

Je **ne peux pas** voir.

426   I cannot see.

le canot, le canoë

427   canoe

le cantaloup

428   cantaloupe

La rivière serpente dans **le canyon**.

429   canyon

la casquette

430   cap

le cap

431   cape

la cape

432   cape

une lettre **majuscule**

A

433   capital

le capitaine du bateau

434   captain

capturer un papillon

435   to capture

la voiture

436   car

La caravane traverse le désert.

437   caravan

les cartes

438   cards

la boîte en **carton**

439   cardboard

L'infirmière **soigne** les malades.

440   to care

Sébastien est **insouciant**.

441   He is careless.

la cargaison d'un avion

442   cargo

un **œillet**

443   carnation

le carnaval

444   carnival

le charpentier

445   carpenter

le tapis

446   carpet

la voiture d'enfant

447   carriage/pram*

la carotte

448   carrot

Le déménageur **porte** une grosse caisse.

449   to carry

la charrette

450   cart

Les vis sont rangées dans **le carton**.

451   carton

découper une tranche de poulet

452   to carve

le coffre

453   case

de l'**argent liquide**

454   cash

des noix d'acajou

455   cashew nuts

le château

456   castle

le chat

457   cat

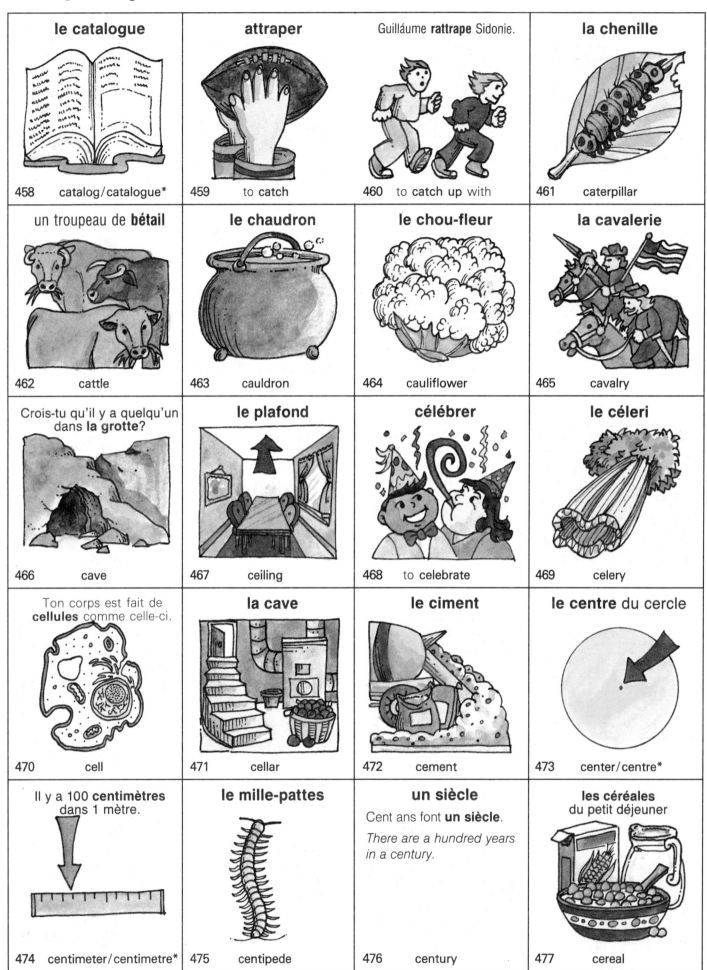

le catalogue
458   catalog/catalogue*

attraper
459   to catch

Guilláume **rattrape** Sidonie.
460   to catch up with

la chenille
461   caterpillar

un troupeau de **bétail**
462   cattle

le chaudron
463   cauldron

le chou-fleur
464   cauliflower

la cavalerie
465   cavalry

Crois-tu qu'il y a quelqu'un dans **la grotte**?
466   cave

le plafond
467   ceiling

célébrer
468   to celebrate

le céleri
469   celery

Ton corps est fait de **cellules** comme celle-ci.
470   cell

la cave
471   cellar

le ciment
472   cement

le centre du cercle
473   center/centre*

Il y a 100 **centimètres** dans 1 mètre.
474   centimeter/centimetre*

le mille-pattes
475   centipede

un siècle
Cent ans font **un siècle**.

There are a hundred years in a century.
476   century

les céréales
du petit déjeuner
477   cereal

certain

Julie est **certaine**
d'avoir raison.
Elle a **certains** sentiments
pour Laurent.

*Julie is certain that she
is right.*
*She has a certain feeling
about Laurent.*

478   certain

le certificat

479   certificate

la chaîne

480   chain

la tronçonneuse

481   chainsaw

la chaise

482   chair

la craie

483   chalk

la championne

484   champion

la monnaie

485   change

le chenal, le canal

487   channel

le douzième **chapitre** du livre

488   chapter

le caractère

Julie a du **caractère**.
Que veut dire ce **caractère**
chinois?

*Julie has a strong
character.*
*What does this Chinese
character mean?*

489   character

changer, se changer

486   to change

le charbon de bois

490   charcoal

le cardon

491   chard

inculper, recharger

La police a **inculpé** Jules
de vol.
Ton jouet s'est arrêté parce
que j'ai oublié de **recharger**
la batterie.

*The police charged Jules
with robbery.*
*Your toy has stopped
because I forgot to charge
the battery.*

492   to **charge**

le char-

493   chariot

le graphique

494   chart

poursuivre

495   to chase

bavarder

496   to chat

un crayon **bon marché**, une couronne chère

497   **cheap** pencil, expensive crown

Éric essaie de tricher.

498   to cheat

vérifier

As-tu **vérifié** ta montre ce matin?

Did you check your watch this morning?

499   to check

la joue

500   cheek

Le fromage est fait avec du lait.

501   cheese

le chèque

502   cheque*/check

les cerises

503   cherries

la poitrine nue

504   chest

les châtaignes, les marrons

505   chestnut

Mâche bien avant d'avaler.

506   to chew

les pois chiches

507   chick peas

le poulet

508   chicken

Charles a **la varicelle**.

509   chicken-pox

Le chef salue les soldats.

510   chief

l'enfant

511   child

un jour **frais**

512   a chilly day

la cheminée

513   chimney

le chimpanzé

514   chimpanzee

le menton

515   chin

la vaisselle

516   china/crockery*

un copeau de bois

517   chip

le ciseau à bois du menuisier

518   chisel

la ciboulette

519   chives

le chocolat

520   chocolate

le chœur, la chorale

521   choir

Etrangler quelqu'un, ce n'est pas une blague.

522   to choke

Claude **s'étrangle** avec un os.

523   to choke on

Lequel des deux dois-je **choisir?**

524   to choose

hacher, couper

525   to chop

les baguettes

526   chopsticks

Le pare-choc de l'auto est en **chrome**.

527   chrome

le chrysanthème

528   chrysanthemum

le morceau de charbon

529   a chunk/lump* of coal

La fumée du **cigare** sent mauvais.

530   cigar

La cigarette est mauvaise pour la santé.

531   cigarette

le cercle

532   circle

le cirque

533   circus

Est-ce que tu vis dans **une** grande **ville?**

534   city

La palourde vit dans sa coquille.

535   clam

L'étau serre les deux planches ensemble.

536   clamp

applaudir

537   to clap

la classe

538　　classroom

Le crabe a **des pinces** puissantes.

539　　claw

---

l'argile

L'argile sert à faire des briques.
L'argile sert aussi à faire des pots.

Clay is used to make bricks.
Clay is also used for making pots.

540　　clay

Elle est toute **propre**.

541　She is all **clean**.

Tante Annie **dessert** la table.

542　　to clear

---

la falaise

543　　cliff

---

grimper, escalader

544　　to climb

---

la clinique

545　　clinic

---

couper, tailler

546　　to clip

---

une pendule

547　　clock

Amandine **ferme** le livre.

548　　to close

Ton **placard** est-il toujours bien rangé?

549　　closet/cupboard*

---

le tissu, le linge

Les vêtements sont faits de **tissu**.
Maman se sert d'**un linge** à vaisselle pour essuyer les assiettes.

Clothes are made of cloth.
Mother uses a dishcloth to wipe the plates.

550　　cloth

---

les vêtements

551　　clothes

---

la corde à linge

552　　clothes line

---

le nuage

553　　cloud

Un trèfle à quatre feuilles porte bonheur.

554　　clover

---

le clown

555　　clown

Thal va à la chasse avec **une massue**.

556　　club

---

l'indice, l'indication

La police a trouvé **un indice** dans cette affaire de vol.
Je vais te donner **une indication**.

The police found a clue to the robbery.
I will give you a clue.

557　　clue

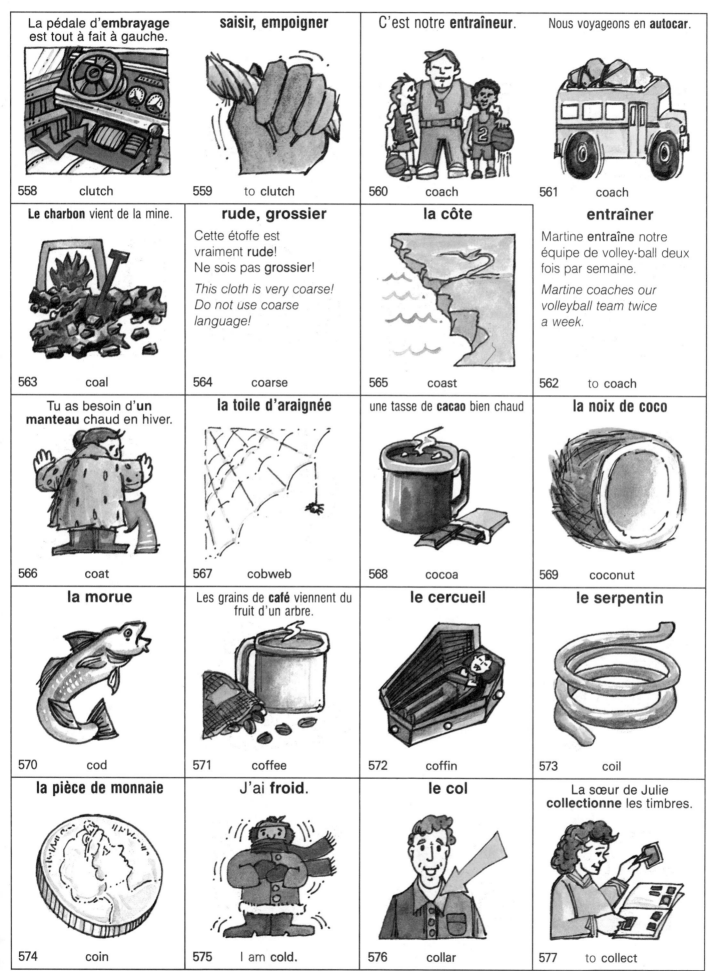

La pédale d'**embrayage** est tout à fait à gauche.

558   clutch

saisir, empoigner

559   to **clutch**

C'est notre **entraîneur**.

560   **coach**

Nous voyageons en **autocar**.

561   **coach**

Le charbon vient de la mine.

563   coal

rude, grossier

Cette étoffe est vraiment **rude**!
Ne sois pas **grossier**!

*This cloth is very coarse!
Do not use coarse
language!*

564   coarse

la côte

565   coast

entraîner

Martine **entraîne** notre équipe de volley-ball deux fois par semaine.

*Martine coaches our
volleyball team twice
a week.*

562   to **coach**

Tu as besoin d'**un manteau** chaud en hiver.

566   coat

la toile d'araignée

567   cobweb

une tasse de **cacao** bien chaud

568   cocoa

la noix de coco

569   coconut

la morue

570   cod

Les grains de **café** viennent du fruit d'un arbre.

571   coffee

le cercueil

572   coffin

le serpentin

573   coil

la pièce de monnaie

574   coin

J'ai **froid**.

575   I am **cold**.

le col

576   collar

La sœur de Julie **collectionne** les timbres.

577   to **collect**

Le collège est une école pour les grands.

578   college

Les voitures **entrent en collision** quand les conducteurs dorment au volant.

579   to collide

la collision

580   collision

Quelle est ta **couleur** préférée?

581   color/colours*

Le poulain est le petit de la jument.

582   colt

deux **colonnes** de pierre

583   column

le peigne

584   comb

Sandra **se peigne** les cheveux.

585   to comb

mélanger les ingrédients

586   combine

venir

Julie **est venue** à la fête en autobus.
Vous **venez** souvent ici?
Dis-lui de **venir** à la maison!

*Julie came to the party by bus.
Do you come here often?
Tell him to come home!*

587   to come

La poignée **s'est détachée**.

588   to come off

Il revient à lui.

589   to come to

confortable

590   comfortable

la virgule

591   comma

commander

592   to command

la communauté

C'est grâce à un effort de la **communauté** que l'école a été construite.
Il y a une piscine au centre **communautaire**.

*Building the school was a community effort.
There is a pool at the community center.*

593   community

deux **compagnons** inséparables

594   companion

Je suis en bonne **compagnie**.

595   I am in good company.

comparer

596   to compare

Ma **boussole** indique le nord.

597   My compass points north.

Jean-Sébastien **compose** une symphonie.

598   to **compose**

le compositeur

599   **composer**

une composition au piano

600   **composition**

un ordinateur

601   computer

Monique se **concentre** sur son travail.

602   to **concentrate**

le concert

603   **concert**

le béton

604   concrete

le chef d'orchestre

605   conductor

le cône

607   **cone**

le cornet de crème glacée

608   ice cream **cone**

la pomme de pin

609   pine **cone**

le chef de train

606   conductor/guard*

L'acrobate est **sûr** de lui.

610   confident

Je suis **un peu perdu**.

611   I am **confused**

féliciter le gagnant

612   to **congratulate**

connecter

613   to **connect**

une consonne

B, c, d, f, g sont des **consonnes**.

B, c, d, f, g are consonants.

614   **consonant**

une agente de police

615   constable

Une constellation a beaucoup d'étoiles.

616   constellation

Il y a sept **continents**.

617   continent

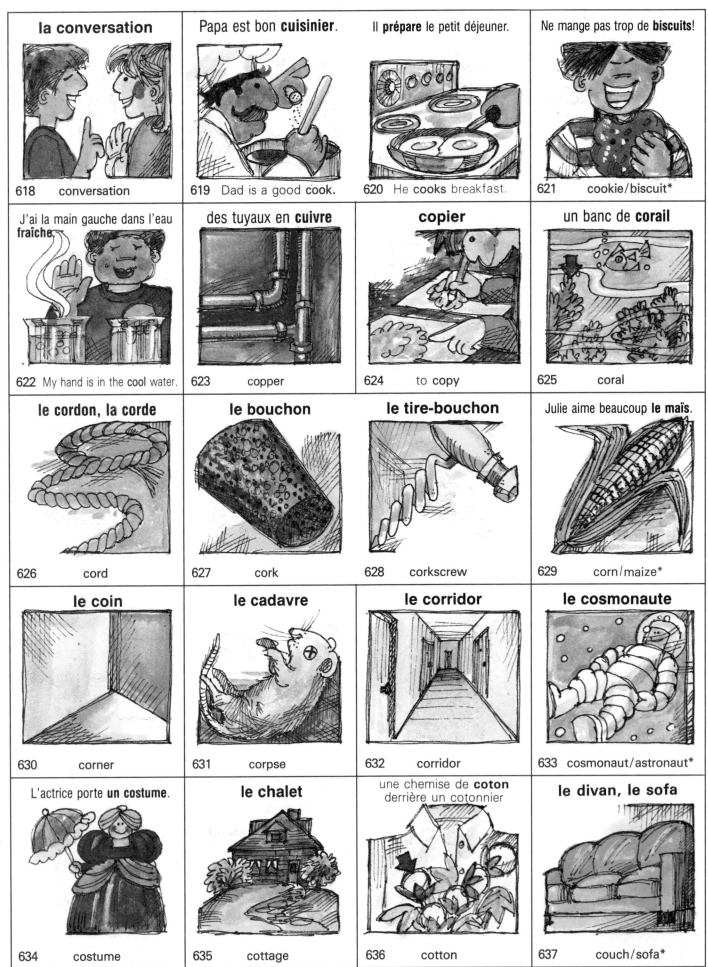

la conversation

618 conversation

Papa est bon **cuisinier**.

619 Dad is a good **cook**.

Il **prépare** le petit déjeuner.

620 He **cooks** breakfast.

Ne mange pas trop de **biscuits**!

621 cookie/biscuit*

J'ai la main gauche dans l'eau **fraîche**.

622 My hand is in the **cool** water.

des tuyaux en **cuivre**

623 copper

copier

624 to copy

un banc de **corail**

625 coral

le cordon, la corde

626 cord

le bouchon

627 cork

le tire-bouchon

628 corkscrew

Julie aime beaucoup **le maïs**.

629 corn/maize*

le coin

630 corner

le cadavre

631 corpse

le corridor

632 corridor

le cosmonaute

633 cosmonaut/astronaut*

L'actrice porte **un costume**.

634 costume

le chalet

635 cottage

une chemise de **coton** derrière un cotonnier

636 cotton

le divan, le sofa

637 couch/sofa*

Amandine **tousse** poliment.	**compter**	**le compteur**	Mets-le sur **le comptoir**!
638 to cough	639 to count	640 counter	641 counter
Est-ce que tu vas souvent à **la campagne**?	Ce **pays**, c'est le Canada.	Maman et papa forment **un couple**.	Il faut du **courage** pour se battre avec les dragons!
642 country	643 country	644 couple	645 courage
le court de tennis	Ma **cousine** est la fille de mon oncle.	**couvrir**	**le couvercle**
646 court	647 My cousin is my uncle's daughter.	648 to cover	649 cover
la vache	Ce garçon est **un poltron**.	**le cow-boy**	**le crabe**
650 cow	651 This boy is a **coward**.	652 cowboy	653 crab
Le vase a **une fissure**.	manger **un craquelin**	**le berceau**	**la grue**
654 crack	655 cracker	656 cradle	657 crane

la grue

658 crane

heurter, tomber avec fracas

659 to crash

Qu'est-ce qu'il y a dans la caisse?

660 crate

ramper

661 to crawl

une écrevisse

662 crayfish

les crayons de couleur

663 crayons

la crème

Papa prend son café avec de la crème.
La crème glacée est très sucrée.

Dad likes cream in his coffee.
Ice cream is very sweet.

664 cream

le pli

665 crease

Quelle étrange créature!

666 creature

le ruisseau

667 creek

l'équipage du navire

668 the crew

le lit d'enfant

669 crib/cot*

le criquet

670 cricket

le criminel

671 criminal

le crocodile

672 crocodile

Les crocus annoncent le printemps!

673 crocus

L'escroc a volé une pomme.

674 crook

Le poteau est **tordu.**

675 crooked post

Le tableau est **penché**, la tour est droite.

676 crooked painting, upright tower

La récolte est belle!

677 crop

la croix

678   cross

Regarde avant de **traverser** la rue!

679   to cross

Le 6 a été **barré**.

680   to cross out

le corbeau, la corneille

681   crow

une foule immense dans un petit espace

682   A big **crowd** in a small space.

la couronne

683   crown

Le roi **couronne** la nouvelle reine.

684   to crown

les miettes

685   crumb

On **écrase** les raisins pour faire du vin.

686   to crush

C'est **la croûte** que Julie préfère!

687   crust

la béquille

688   crutch

pleurer

689   to cry

une boule de **cristal**

690   crystal

un ourson

691   cub

le cube

692   cube

le coucou

693   cuckoo

le concombre

694   cucumber

le poignet de chemise

695   cuff

la tasse de thé

696   cup

La confiture est dans **le buffet**.

697   cupboard

le bord du trottoir

698   curb/kerb*

Je suis guéri.

699   I am cured.

boucler, friser

700   to curl

les cheveux **bouclés, frisés**

701   curly

Hélène est **curieuse**.

702   curious

la groseille

703   currant

Le courant est fort.

704   current

les rideaux

705   curtains

la courbe

706   curve

le coussin

707   cushion

le client

708   customer

trancher, couper

709   to cut

Sandra est **mignonne**.

712   cute/sweet*

les couverts

713   cutlery

le cycle

714   cycle

couper la route

710   to cut in

le cylindre

715   cylinder

les cymbales

716   cymbals

le cyprès

717   cypress

Découpe la poupée en papier!

711   to cut out

Les jonquilles fleurissent au printemps.

718   daffodil

le poignard

719   dagger

Milou apporte **le quotidien.**

720   daily

la laiterie

721   dairy

Effeuillons ensemble **la marguerite.**

722   daisy

le barrage sur la rivière

723   dam

endommagé, abîmé

724   damaged

mouillé, humide

725   damp

danser

726   to dance

la danseuse

727   dancer

Le pissenlit est une mauvaise herbe.

728   dandelion

Attention! **Danger.**

729   danger

Luc n'a pas peur dans **le noir.**

730   dark

le jeu de **fléchettes**

731   dart

le tableau de bord

732   dashboard

Quelle est **la date** aujourd'hui?

733   date

C'est ma **fille** Pénélope.

734   daughter

le début d'**une** belle **journée**

735   the start of a nice **day**

La souris est **morte.**

736   **dead** mouse

sourd

737　　deaf

cher

Mon **cher** ami.
Chère maman, il fait très froid ici et j'ai oublié d'apporter mon manteau.

My dear friend.
Dear Mother, it is quite cold here and I forgot to bring my coat.

738　　dear

Décembre est le dernier moïs de l'année.

739　　December

décider

Julie n'arrive pas à **décider** comment s'habiller.
Peut-être Maman va-t-elle devoir **décider** pour elle.

Julie cannot decide what to wear.
Mother may have to decide for her.

740　　to decide

le pont d'un navire

741　　deck

Le pirate **décore** son arbre de Noël.

742　　to decorate

la décoration

743　　decoration

Albert évite le côté **profond** de la piscine.

744　　deep end

Les cerfs vivent dans les forêts.

745　　deer

livrer

746　　to deliver

bosseler, cabosser

747　　to dent

la dentiste

748　　dentist

le grand magasin

749　　department store

le désert

750　　desert

Qui a mis ce **bureau** dans le désert?

751　　desk

le dessert

752　　dessert

démolir, détruire

753　　to destroy

le contre-torpilleur

754　　destroyer

Le détective enquête.

755　　detective

Le matin, les feuilles sont couvertes de **rosée**.

756　　dew

la diagonale
757   diagonal

le diagramme
758   diagram

le diamant
759   diamond

Bébé a besoin de **couches**.
760   diaper/nappy*

Suzanne tient **un journal**.
761   diary

Elle vérifie un mot dans **le dictionnaire**.
762   dictionary

mourir
763   to die

différence
Tous les gens naissent égaux, en dépit **des différences** qui les séparent.

All people are born equal despite the differences among them.
764   difference

des gens **différents**
765   **different** people

creuser
766   to dig

Le serpent **digère** un éléphant.
767   The snake **digests** an elephant.

La pièce est **sombre**.
768   dim

Julie a **des fossettes**.
769   dimple

le canot, le youyou
770   dinghy

la salle à manger
771   dining room

le dîner à la chandelle
772   dinner

le dinosaure
773   dinosaur

la direction à suivre
774   direction

Papa a marché dans de **la saleté**.
775   dirt

Ses pantalons sont **sales**.
776   dirty

Ils sont en désaccord.	La pomme **est disparue**.	Cet incendie est **un** véritable **désastre**.	Le navigateur **découvre** une île.
777 to disagree	778 to disappear	779 disaster	780 to discover
discuter	**la maladie**	Julie porte **un déguisement**.	Julie, où es-tu? Viens vite faire **la vaisselle**.
781 to discuss	782 disease	783 disguise	784 dishes
une personne **malhonnête**	**l'eau de vaisselle**	Anna **déteste** les légumes.	Le comprimé va se **dissoudre** dans l'eau.
785 a dishonest person	786 dishwater	787 to dislike	788 to dissolve
la distance entre les deux arbres	un arbre **lointain**	**le district** où j'habite	creuser **un fossé**
789 distance between two trees	790 a distant tree	791 district	792 ditch
plonger	**diviser**	J'ai des vertiges.	Que dois-je **faire**?
793 to dive	794 to divide	795 I feel **dizzy**.	796 What shall I do?

le bassin	797 dock
le médecin	798 doctor
le chien	799 dog
la poupée	800 doll
le dauphin	801 dolphin
le dôme	802 dome
Cet **âne** porte un lourd fardeau.	803 donkey
la porte	804 door
la poignée de porte	805 doorknob
double	806 double
la pâte	807 dough
La colombe est le symbole de la paix.	808 dove
Julie a un oreiller en **duvet**.	809 down
sommeiller	810 to doze
une douzaine d'œufs	811 dozen
Ne **traîne** pas ton sac par terre!	812 to drag
le dragon	813 dragon
la libellule	814 dragonfly
le drain	815 drain/plug hole*
Robert **dessine** bien.	816 to draw

Relevez **le pont-levis**!

817 drawbridge

Les chaussettes de Julie ne sont pas dans **le tiroir**.

818 drawer

un beau **rêve**

819 a nice **dream**

Je **rêve** de moutons.

820 I **dream** of sheep.

la robe

821 dress

s'habiller

822 to **dress**

Les chaussettes de Julie sont peut-être dans **la commode**.

823 dresser/chest of drawers*

baver

824 to **dribble**

Quelle tristesse de **dériver** sans fin!

825 to **drift**

Patricia **perce** des trous.

826 to **drill**

la perceuse

827 drill

la boisson

828 drink

Le robinet **fuit**.

830 to **drip**

Je **conduis** prudemment.

831 I **drive** carefully.

Le conducteur a été imprudent.

832 crazy **driver**

Mistigris **boit** son lait.

829 to **drink**

la bruine

La **bruine** est une pluie très fine.

Drizzle is a very fine rain.

833 drizzle

Mistigris **bave** d'envie.

834 to **drool**

une goutte de sirop

835 drop

laisser tomber

836 to **drop**

Julien **est passé voir** Dominique.

837   to drop in

Papa **dépose** le chat chez le vétérinaire.

838   Dad **drops off** the cat at the vet.

abandonner la course

839   to drop out

J'ai sommeil.

840   I feel **drowsy.**

le tambour

841   drum

sec

842   dry

sécher

843   to dry

le nettoyeur à sec

844   dry cleaner

Mets le linge dans **la sécheuse!**

845   dryer

la duchesse

846   duchess

le canard

847   duck

le duel

848   duel

le duc

849   duke

le dépotoir

850   dump

déverser

851   to dump

le camion-benne

852   dumptruck/lorry*

Le prisonnier est enfermé dans **le donjon**.

853   dungeon

le crépuscule

854   dusk

Jeanne enlève **la poussière** avec son plumeau.

855   dust

le nain

856   dwarf

E

Chaque lapin a une carotte.

857 **Each** rabbit has a carrot.

Les aigles sont devenus rares; il faut les protéger.

858 eagle

une oreille

859 ear

le soleil **matinal**

860 early

gagner, mériter

Maman **gagne** un bon salaire.
Julie a bien **mérité** des vacances.

Mother earns a good wage.
Julie has earned a holiday.

861 to earn

la Terre

862 Earth

creuser **la terre**

863 earth

le tremblement de terre

864 earthquake

le chevalet du peintre

865 easel

L'est est opposé à l'ouest.

866 east

C'est **facile** de nager.

867 Swimming is **easy.**

manger

868 to eat

prendre son petit déjeuner

869 to eat breakfast

déjeuner

870 to eat lunch

dîner, souper

871 to eat dinner/supper*

un écho

872 echo

une éclipse solaire

873 eclipse

L'arbre est **au bord de** la falaise.

874 The tree is at the **edge.**

une anguille

875 eel

La poule a pondu **un œuf**.

876   egg

L'aubergine est violette.

877   eggplant/aubergine*

huit insectes

878   eight

le huitième poisson

879   eighth

Éric joue avec **un élastique**.

880   elastic

le coude

881   elbow

une élection

On tient **des élections** pour choisir un gouvernement. Qui a remporté **l'élection**?

Elections are held to choose the government. Who won the election?

882   election

un électricien

883   electrician

l'électricité

884   electricity

un éléphant

885   elephant

Béatrice attend **l'ascenseur**.

886   elevator/lift*

un élan

887   elk

un orme

888   elm

embarrasser, déconcerter

889   to embarrass

serrer dans ses bras

890   to embrace

la broderie

891   embroidery

une urgence

892   emergency

La boîte est **vide**.

893   The jar is **empty**.

C'est **la fin** de la route.

894   This is the **end**.

Un jour ils ne seront peut-être plus **ennemis**.

895   enemies

le moteur de l'auto

896   engine

le conducteur du train

897   engineer/engine driver*

savourer, apprécier

898   to enjoy

un dinosaure **énorme**

899   enormous dinosaur

C'est **assez**.

900   That is **enough**.

Milou **entre** par la porte.

901   to **enter**

une entrée

902   entrance

une enveloppe

903   envelope

des boucs de force **égale**

904   equal

L'équateur divise la Terre en deux hémisphères.

905   equator

la commission, la course

Julie fait **une commission** pour Papa.
Elle a beaucoup de **courses** à faire ce matin.

Julie is running an errand for Dad.
She has many errands this morning.

906   errand

un escalier roulant

907   escalator

La souris **s'enfuit**.

908   to **escape**

L'Europe est un continent.

909   Europe

Une évaporation se produit à cause de la chaleur du soleil.

910   evaporation

Quatre est un chiffre **pair**.

$n \times 2 = ?$

911   Four is an **even** number.

une surface **lisse**

912   an **even** surface

Le sapin est **un arbre à feuilles persistantes**.

913   evergreen

chaque

Julie fait son lit presque **chaque** matin.
Est-ce que Maman doit lui rappeler de le faire **chaque** matin?

Julie makes her bed almost every morning.
Must Mother tell her every morning?

914   every

un examen facile

915   exam

examiner à la loupe

916   to examine

un exemple

Parfois, Julie ne montre pas **le** bon **exemple**.
Il est plus facile de comprendre avec **un exemple**.

*Sometimes, Julie does not set a good example.
Things are easier to understand when you give an example.*

917   example

le point d'exclamation

918   exclamation mark

Pardonnez-moi, excusez-moi!

919   Excuse me!

Corinne **fait des exercices**.

920   to exercise

exister

Exister, c'est être.
Les dinosaures n'**existent** plus.

*To exist is to be.
Dinosaurs no longer exist.*

921   to exist

sortir

922   to exit/leave*

gonfler un ballon

923   to expand

attendre, s'attendre à

Nous vous **attendons** à deux heures.
Papa **s'attend à** ce que tu sois sage.

*We expect you at two o'clock.
Dad expects you to be good.*

924   to expect

Une montre **chère** coûte beaucoup d'argent.

925   expensive

faire **une expérience**

926   experiment

une experte

927   expert

Serge **explique** à Milou qu'il doit obéir.

928   to explain

L'aventurier **explore** la jungle.

929   to explore

une explosion

930   explosion

un extincteur

931   extinguisher

un œil

932   eye

le sourcil

933   eyebrow

les lunettes

934   eyeglasses/spectacles*

les cils

935   eyelash

la **fable** de la cigale et de la fourmi

936   fable

le visage, la face

937   face

une usine

938   factory

Thomas **a échoué** à son examen.

939   to fail

tomber en panne

940   to fail

la foire

941   fair

La fée exaucera ton vœu.

942   fairy

la foi, la confiance

Nous avons **confiance** en toi.
Julie l'a accepté de bonne **foi**.

We have faith in you.
Julie accepted it in good faith.

943   faith

le **faux** tableau

944   fake painting

En **automne**, les feuilles tombent.

945   fall/autumn*

tomber

946   to fall

C'était une **fausse** alerte!

949   false alarm

la famille

950   family

tomber par terre

947   to fall down

faire une chute

948   to fall off

Brigitte est une **célèbre** actrice.

951   famous actress

le ventilateur

952   fan

une tenue **élégante, habillée**

953   fancy clothes

le croc

954   fang

La ville est loin.	**Adieu!**	**la ferme**	**le fermier, l'agriculteur**
955 The city is **far** away.	956 Farewell !	957 farm	958 farmer
rapide	**J'attache** ma ceinture.	**gros, gras**	Ce poison est **mortel**.
959 fast	960 I **fasten** my seatbelt.	961 fat	962 fatal
le père	**Le robinet** fuit.	À qui **la faute**?	**la faveur, le service** Puis-je vous demander **une faveur**? Julie est gentille et elle aime rendre **service**. *Can I ask you a favor/favour*?* *Julie is kind and likes doing people favors/favours*.*
963 father	964 faucet/tap*	965 Whose **fault** is it?	966 favor/favour*
ma saveur **favorite**	**craindre** le pire	**le banquet**	**la plume** d'un oiseau
967 favorite/favourite*	968 to **fear** the worst	969 feast	970 feather
Février est le deuxième mois de l'année.	**nourrir, alimenter**	Je **me sens** bien.	**La femelle** pond les œufs.
971 February	972 to feed	973 I **feel** well.	974 female

la clôture	**une aile d'auto**	**la fougère**	Paul et Anne prennent **le traversier**.
975 fence	976 fender/wing*	977 fern	978 ferry
le festival	Patrick a de **la fièvre**.	**Peu** de gens sont venus.	**le champ**
979 festival	980 fever	981 Few people came.	982 field
Alice est **la cinquième**.	**se battre, se bagarrer**	Régine se **lime** les ongles.	**remplir, emplir**
983 fifth	984 to fight	985 to file	986 to fill
Luce a **un film** pour son appareil-photo.	**sale, dégoûtant**	**la nageoire** d'un requin	**remplir, faire le plein**
988 film	989 filthy	990 fin	987 to fill up
L'agent lui donne **une amende**.	Je vais **bien**.	**le doigt**	**une empreinte digitale**
991 fine	992 I am fine.	993 finger	994 fingerprint

Joëlle **finit** première.

995   to finish

Le sapin a des aiguilles.

996   fir

le feu

997   fire

la voiture de pompiers

998   fire engine

la sortie de secours

999   fire escape

Les **pétards** peuvent être dangereux!

1000   firecracker/banger*

le pompier

1001   firefighter

un **âtre**, la cheminée, le foyer

1002   fireplace

ferme

Julie a une poignée de main **ferme**.
La décision de Papa est **ferme**. Thomas n'aura pas d'autre glace!

Julie has a firm handshake. Dad's decision is firm, Thomas cannot have another ice cream.

1003   firm

le premier de la file

1004   first

le poisson

1005   fish

Jean **pêche** dans la rivière.

1006   to fish

un hameçon

1007   fishhook

le poing

1008   fist

cinq

1009   five

Crois-tu qu'il va savoir **réparer** la voiture?

1010   to fix

le drapeau des pirates

1011   flag

Les flocons de neige tombent du ciel.

1012   flake

la flamme

1013   flame

Cuicui **bat** des ailes.

1014   to flap

le feu de signal	**le flash**	**la lampe de poche**	**le flacon**
1015 flare	1016 flash	1017 flashlight/torch*	1018 flask

plat	Maman **aplatit** la pâte avec un rouleau.	Quel **parfum** préfères-tu?	Zap a **une puce**.
1019 flat	1020 to flatten	1021 flavor/flavour*	1022 flea

Luc **s'enfuit** à belles jambes!	**la toison** du mouton	Il est bien **en chair**.	**flotter**
1023 to flee	1024 fleece	1025 flesh	1026 . to float

un vol d'oiseaux	**une inondation**	**le sol**, **le plancher**	Le boulanger fait du pain avec de **la farine**.
1027 flock	1028 flood	1029 floor	1030 flour

Le sang **coule** dans le tube.	**la fleur**	Luc a attrapé **la grippe**.	**le duvet, la peluche**
1031 to flow	1032 flower	1033 flu	1034 fluff

La limonade est **un liquide**.

1035   fluid

la mouche

1036   fly

la braguette des pantalons

1037   fly

Les oiseaux et les avions **volent**.

1038   to fly

la mousse

1039   foam

Impossible de voir clairement avec ce **brouillard**!

1040   fog

Plier comme indiqué.

1041   to fold

L'oie **suit** Jeannot partout.

1042   to follow

la nourriture

1043   food

le pied

1044   foot

le ballon **de football**

1045   American football

une empreinte de pas dans la neige

1046   footprint

J'entends **des pas** derrière moi.

1047   footsteps

pour

Tous **pour** un et un **pour** tous.
Pour le meilleur ou **pour** le pire.

One for all and all for one
For better or for worse

1048   for

Il **force** la porte.

1049   to force

le front

1050   forehead

La forêt est pleine d'animaux.

1051   forest

oublier

Notre chien **oublie** son nom.
Papa **a oublié** d'acheter du lait.

Our dog forgets his name.
Dad forgot to buy milk.

1052   to forget

pardonner

Je te **pardonne** si tu promets d'être gentil.
Julie **a pardonné** à son chien d'avoir mangé la poupée.

I forgive you if you promise to be good.
Julie forgave her dog for eating the doll.

1053   to forgive

la fourchette

1054   fork

le chariot élévateur

1055   forklift

la forme

1056   form/tailor's dummy*

Les soldats sont dans **le fort**.

1057   fort

de l'avant, hardi

Va **de l'avant** jusqu'à ce que tu arrives à la porte. Julie pense qu'il est trop **hardi**.

Go forward until you reach the door.
Julie thinks he is too forward.

1058   forward

le fossile d'un poisson

1059   fossil

une odeur **infecte**

1060   foul odor/odour*

les fondations de la maison

1061   foundation

la fontaine

1062   fountain

Le renard est un animal rusé.

1063   fox

⅛ est **une fraction**.

1064   fraction

L'œuf est **fragile**.

1065   fragile

le cadre

1066   frame

Est-ce que tu as **des taches de rousseur**?

1067   freckle

L'oiseau est **libre**.

1068   free

geler, congeler

1069   to freeze

Une pomme encore toute **fraîche** de l'arbre.

1070   fresh

vendredi

Une fois **le vendredi** fini, plus d'école jusqu'au lundi!

Friday means no more school until Monday!

1071   Friday

le réfrigérateur

1072   fridge

des amis

1073   friends

Charlotte l'**a effrayé**.

1074   to frighten

la grenouille

1075   frog

Je viens **de** la planète Mars.

1076   I am **from** Mars.

l'avant

1077   front

La vitre est couverte de **givre**.

1078   frost

froncer les sourcils

1079   to **frown**

Les fruits sont bien meilleurs que les bonbons.

1080   fruit

frire

1081   to **fry**

la poêle à frire

1082   frying pan

Les voitures ont besoin d'**essence**.

1083   Cars need **fuel**.

plein

1084   full

avoir du plaisir, s'amuser

1085   having **fun**

la caisse de charité

1086   charity **fund**

les funérailles

1087   funeral

un entonnoir

1088   funnel

drôle, amusant

Maman ne trouve pas ça **drôle**.
Une chose **amusante** s'est passée à l'école aujourd'hui.

Mother does not think that is funny.
A funny thing happened at school today.

1089   funny

Un manteau de **fourrure** en été!

1090   fur coat

la chaudière, le calorifère

1092   furnace/boiler*

le mobilier

1093   furniture

Plus de lumière! **Les fusibles** ont sauté.

1094   fuse

un chat **à longs poils**

1091   furry

G

un grand vent

1095   gale

la galerie d'art

1096   gallery

Un cheval peut trotter ou **galoper**.

1097   to gallop

Noémie aime **les jeux**.

1098   game

Le jars est le mâle de l'oie.

1099   gander

une bande de voleurs

1100   gang

Julie a un **vide** entre les deux dents de devant.

1101   gap

L'auto est dans **le garage**.

1102   garage

les ordures, les détritus

1103   garbage/rubbish*

la poubelle, la boîte à ordures

1104   garbage can/rubbish bin*

le potager

1105   vegetable **garden**

se gargariser

1106   to gargle

L'ail a un goût très fort.

1107   garlic

la jarretière

1108   garter

le gaz

Le ballon était rempli de **gaz**.
Certains **gaz** sont plus légers que l'air.

The balloon was filled with gas.
Some gases are lighter than air.

1109   gas

l'essence

1110   gas/petrol*

la pédale d'accélérateur

1111   gas pedal/accelerator*

la pompe à essence

1112   gas/petrol pump*

la station-service

1113   gas/petrol station*

le portail	Louise **cueille** des fleurs.	**les engrenages**	Le diamant est **une pierre précieuse**.
1114 gate	1115 to gather	1116 gears	1117 gem
le général	un ami **généreux**	une personne **douce, gentille**	Papa est **un vrai gentilhomme**.
1118 general	1119 a generous friend	1120 a gentle person	1121 gentleman
un **vrai** cochon	Nous étudions tous **la géographie**.	**le géranium**	**la gerbille**
1122 a genuine pig	1123 geography	1124 geranium	1125 gerbil
Les germes provoquent des maladies.	Mistigris! **Attrape** cette souris!	Je veux que tu me le rendes.	Julie **entre** dans la piscine.
1126 germ	1127 Get that mouse!	1128 I want to **get** it **back**.	1129 to **get in** the pool
Julie **descend** de l'autobus.	Elle **monte** dans le tramway.	Elle **se débarrasse** des ordures.	Mais d'abord, elle **se lève**.
1130 to **get off**	1131 to **get on**	1132 to **get rid of**	1133 to **get up**

As-tu peur **des fantômes**?	**le géant**	**le cadeau** de Rosalie	une baleine **gigantesque**
1134 ghost	1135 giant	1136 gift	1137 gigantic

avoir un petit rire nerveux	**les ouïes, les branchies**	**Le gingembre** est une épice.	un bonhomme en **pain d'épice**
1138 to giggle	1139 gills	1140 ginger	1141 gingerbread

le gitan et sa roulotte	**la girafe**	Suzon est **une fille**.	Suzon **donne** un parapluie à Anne.
1142 gipsy	1143 giraffe	1144 girl	1145 to give

le glacier	Je suis **content**.	**le verre**	Anne **rend** le parapluie.
1148 glacier	1149 I am glad.	1150 glass	1146 to give back

Est-ce que tu portes **des lunettes**?	**glisser**	**un verre** d'eau	Je **me rends**!
1152 glasses	1153 to glide	1151 glass	1147 I give up!

Le planeur n'a pas de moteur.

1154   glider

des gants

1155   gloves

La colle tient bien!

1156   glue

aller, partir

1157   to go

le but

1161   goal

la chèvre

1162   goat

les lunettes protectrices

1163   goggles

Il **descend** travailler.

1158   to go down

le lingot d'**or**

1164   gold

le poisson rouge

1165   goldfish

Oncle Jean joue au **golf**.

1166   golf

Milou **entre** dans sa niche.

1159   to go in

Comme c'est **bon**!

1167   good

Au revoir Maman!

1168   Goodbye!

une oie

1169   goose

Jacques **grimpe** le long du haricot géant.

1160   to go up

les groseilles

1170   gooseberry

Elle pense avoir une coiffure **ravissante**.

1171   gorgeous

le gorille

1172   gorilla

gouverner

Le gouvernement **gouverne** le pays.
Ce n'est pas facile de **gouverner** un pays.

The government governs the country.
It is not easy to govern a country.

1173   to **govern**

le gouvernement

Le gouvernement est élu par les citoyens.
Le papa de Julie travaille pour le gouvernement.

The government is elected by the people.
Julie's Dad works for the government

1174   government

Luc s'est emparé de la glace de Lucie et il sera puni.

1175   to grab

Il est très aimable.

1176   He is very gracious.

Je suis en troisième année.

1177   grade / form*

Avec le grain, on·fait de la farine.

1178   grain

1000 grammes = 1 kilogramme

1179   gram

---

le petit-fils

1180   grandchild

---

le grand-père

1181   grandfather

La grand-mère de Julie aime faire des gâteaux.

1182   grandmother

Le granit est une roche dure.

1183   granite

---

accorder

Je t'accorde dix jours de congé.
La fée t'accordera trois vœux.

I grant you ten days' leave of absence.
The good fairy will grant you three wishes.

1184   to grant

---

une grappe de raisin

1185   grapes

---

le pamplemousse

1186   grapefruit

---

le graphique, le diagramme

1187   graph

L'herbe est verte.

1188   grass

---

la sauterelle

1189   grasshopper

---

la râpe

1190   grater

---

la tombe

1191   grave

---

le gravier au bord de la route

1192   gravel

La gravité fait tomber les pommes.

1193   Gravity makes apples fall.

paître, brouter

1194   to graze

La graisse empêchera la porte de grincer.

1195   grease

un jouet **superbe**

1196   a great toy

avide, cupide

1197   greedy

vert

1198   green

le haricot vert

1199   green bean

la serre

1200   greenhouse

saluer

1201   to greet

La nuit, tous les chats sont **gris**.

1202   grey*/gray

griller

1203   to grill

sale, barbouillé

1204   grimy

Marc **a un grand sourire**.

1205   to grin

hacher, moudre

1206   to grind/to mince*

saisir, agripper

1207   to grip

gémir, geindre

1208   to groan

L'épicier renseigne la cliente.

1209   grocer

le marié et la mariée

1211   groom

Le palefrenier s'occupe des chevaux.

1212   groom

Patricia **se fait belle**.

1213   to groom

faire **des courses d'épicerie**

1210   shopping for groceries

la rainure

1214   groove

choquant, dégoûtant

1215   gross/disgusting*

le sol, la terre

1216   ground

la marmotte

1217   groundhog

le groupe

1218   group

grandir, pousser

1219   to grow

grogner, gronder

1220   to growl

un adulte

1221   grown-up

garder

1222   to guard

Attends! Laisse-moi **deviner**.

1223   to guess

Il fait entrer son **invité**.

1224   guest

Il le **guide** vers sa chambre.

1225   to guide

coupable

Julie dit qu'elle n'a pas volé les bonbons, elle n'est pas **coupable**.
Alors, qui est **coupable** du vol de bonbons?

Julie says she did not steal the candies, she is not guilty.
So who is guilty of stealing the candies?

1226   guilty

le cochon d'Inde

1227   guinea pig

Pablo joue de **la guitare**.

1228   guitar

le golfe du Mexique

1229   Gulf of Mexico

Les mouettes vivent au bord de l'eau.

1230   gull

Brosse-toi les dents et **les gencives**.

1231   gum

C'est vilain de mâcher de **la gomme**.

1232   gum/chewing gum*

L'eau coule dans **le caniveau**.

1233   gutter

Fumer est **une** mauvaise **habitude**.

1234   bad habit

un aiglefin

1235   haddock

une tempête de **grêle**

1236   hail

La sœur de Julie a **les cheveux** drus.

1237   hair

la brosse à cheveux

1238   hairbrush

le coiffeur

1239   hairdresser

un sèche-cheveux encombrant

1240   hairdryer

Veux-tu l'autre **moitié**?

1241   half

le vestibule, l'entrée

1242   hall

l'Halloween

1243   Halloween/Hallowe'en*

le corridor, le couloir

1244   hallway/corridor*

Le soldat **fait halte** devant la porte.

1245   to halt

le marteau

1246   hammer

Lucien **martèle** le morceau de bois.

1247   to hammer

le hamac

1248   hammock

un hamster

1249   hamster

les cinq doigts de **la main**

1250   hand

remettre, distribuer

1251   to hand out

le frein à main

1252   hand brake

les menottes

1253   handcuffs

un handicap

Être aveugle, c'est
un handicap.
Tout **handicap** peut être
surmonté.

*Being blind is a handicap.
People can overcome
any handicap.*

1254   handicap

la poignée

1255   handle

la rampe de l'escalier

1256   handrail

Jerôme se trouve **beau**.

1257   handsome

Une personne **adroite**
de ses mains.

1258   handy person

Suspends le tableau droit!

1259   to hang

Il **se cramponne**.

1260   to hang on

le hangar à avions

1262   hangar

Mets ta veste sur **un cintre**!

1263   hanger

le mouchoir

1264   handkerchief

Simon **accroche** le cintre.

1261   to hang up

Les accidents **arrivent**.

1265   Accidents happen.

Il est **heureux**.

1266   He is happy.

Les bateaux sont dans **le port**.

1267   harbor/harbour*

La pile de briques
est trop **dure**.

1268   hard

le lièvre

1269   hare

Ce n'est pas bien de **faire
du mal** aux animaux!

1270   to harm

un harmonica

1271   harmonica

La bride fait partie du
harnais du cheval.

1272   harness

la harpe	un hiver **rigoureux**	Joseph **moissonne** le blé.	**le chapeau**
1273 harp	1274 a **harsh** winter	1275 to **harvest**	1276 hat
Ce poussin vient d'**éclore**.	**la hachette**	**tirer, transporter**	une maison **hantée**
1277 to **hatch**	1278 hatchet	1279 to **haul**	1280 **haunted** house
Marie **a** la poupée que veut Anna!	**le faucon**	**le foin** pour les chevaux	**La brume** rend l'air brumeux.
1281 to **have**	1282 hawk	1283 hay	1284 **Haze** makes for a hazy day.
le noisetier	**La noisette** est le fruit du noisetier.	**la tête**	J'ai **un mal de tête**.
1285 hazel	1286 hazelnut	1287 head	1288 I have a **headache**.
un appui-tête	Sa jambe **sera** bientôt **guérie**.	une fleur **saine**	**un tas** d'ordures
1289 headrest	1290 to **heal**	1291 **healthy** flower	1292 heap/pile*

J'entends une voix.

1293　I **hear** a voice.

Le cœur bat dans la poitrine.

1294　**heart**

chauffer, faire chauffer

1295　to **heat**

le radiateur

1296　**heater**/radiator*

soulever

1297　to **heave**

le paradis

1298　**heaven**

un éléphant lourd

1299　one **heavy** elephant

Pépé a taillé la haie.

1300　**hedge**

Le hérisson a des piquants.

1301　**hedgehog**

le talon

1302　**heel**

un hélicoptère

1303　**helicopter**

L'enfer n'est pas trop chaud pour ce diable.

1304　**hell**

bonjour, salut

1305　**hello**

la barre, le gouvernail

1306　**helm**

Le soldat porte un casque.

1307　**helmet**

Maman aide Papa à réparer l'auto.

1308　to **help**

Un bébé est si impuissant!

1309　**helpless**

le bord, un ourlet

1310　**hem**

La terre a deux hémisphères.

1311　**hemisphere**

la poule

1312　**hen**

Un heptagone a sept côtés.

1313　heptagon

des herbes

1314　herbs

un troupeau de bétail

1315　herd

Viens **ici!**

1316　Come here!

Un ermite vit seul.

1317　hermit

le héros

1318　hero

une héroïne

1319　heroine

un hareng

1320　herring

Paul **hésite** à plonger.

1321　to hesitate

Un hexagone a six côtés.

1322　hexagon

Les ours **hibernent** en hiver.

1323　to hibernate

avoir le hoquet, hoqueter

1324　to hiccup/hiccough*

la peau, le cuir

1325　hide

Sidonie **se cache**.

1326　to hide

la cachette

1327　hiding-place

une **haute** montagne

1328　a high mountain

un grand immeuble

1329　highrise/tower block*

une école secondaire, un lycée

1330　high school/secondary school*

une grande route, une autoroute

1331　highway/motorway*

détourner un avion

1332　to hijack a plane

le sommet de **la colline**

1333   hill

la charnière

1334   hinge

les pattes **arrière**

1335   hind legs

la main sur **la hanche**

1336   hand on hip

un hippopotame

1337   hippopotamus

J'étudie **l'histoire**.

1338   I study **history**.

frapper, cogner

1339   to hit

Les abeilles vivent dans **la ruche**.

1340   hive

amasser, accumuler

1341   to hoard

la voix **enrouée, rauque**

1342   hoarse voice

un passe-temps, une marotte

1343   hobby

Mon frère joue au **hockey**.

1344   hockey/ice hockey*

la houe, la binette

1347   hoe

Julie **tient** Tigré sur ses genoux.

1348   to **hold**

Julie ne devrait pas le **maintenir à terre**!

1349   to hold down

la rondelle de hockey

1345   hockey puck

le trou

1350   hole

Oncle Jules a bien mérité **ses vacances** au bord de l'eau.

1351   holiday

Des écureuils vivent dans cet arbre **creux**.

1352   hollow tree

le bâton de hockey

1346   hockey stick

Le houx a des baies.

1353   holly

Il y a des pays où les vaches sont **sacrées**.

1354   a **holy** cow

Les écureuils sont **à la maison**.

1355   home

Luc fait ses **devoirs**.

1356   homework

Est-il **honnête**?

1357   Is he honest?

Les ours sont friands de **miel**.

1358   honey

le rayon de miel

1359   honeycomb

le melon vert

1360   honeydew melon

klaxonner

1361   to honk

Quel **honneur** d'obtenir un diplôme!

1362   honor/honour*

Le manteau de Julie a **un capuchon**.

1363   hood

Le moteur est sous **le capot**.

1364   hood/bonnet*

le sabot du cheval

1365   hoof

un hameçon

1366   hook

sauter à travers **un cerceau**

1367   jump through a **hoop**

sauter, sautiller

1368   to hop

J'**espère** gagner.

1369   I hope to win.

C'est **sans espoir**! Il ne saura jamais monter!

1370   hopeless

Aude joue à **la marelle**.

1371   hopscotch/hop-scotch*

Le soleil se lève à l'**horizon**.

1372   horizon

en position **horizontale**	**un avertisseur, un klaxon**	**le cor** d'harmonie	**la corne**
1373 horizontal	1374 horn	1375 French **horn**	1376 horn
Le frelon pique avec son dard.	**le cheval**	**Le raifort** est piquant.	**le fer à cheval**
1377 hornet	1378 horse	1379 horseradish	1380 horseshoe
le tuyau d'arrosage	**un hôpital**	Il fait **chaud!**	C'est **piquant!** J'ai la bouche en feu!
1381 hose	1382 hospital	1383 hot	1384 hot
En voyage, nous dormons à **l'hôtel**.	Il y a soixante minutes dans **une heure**.	**le sablier**	**le piment**
1386 hotel	1387 hour	1388 hourglass	1385 hot pepper
la maison	**un aéroglisseur**	Je vais te montrer **comment** faire.	Le chien **hurle** dans la nuit.
1389 house	1390 hovercraft	1391 I will show you **how**.	1392 to howl

un enjoliveur de roue
1393   hub cap

les airelles
1394   huckleberry

se serrer les uns contre les autres
1395   to huddle

L'éléphant est **énorme**.
1396   huge

la coque du navire
1397   hull

un oiseau-mouche
1398   hummingbird

Le chameau a deux **bosses**.
1399   hump

cent
1400   hundred

Elle **a faim**.
1401   She is **hungry**.

Joël **chasse** avec un fusil.
1402   to hunt

lancer
1403   to hurl

Qui donne un nom aux **ouragans**?
1404   hurricane

se dépêcher
1405   to hurry

Mon poignet me **fait mal**.
1406   My wrist **hurts**.

Édouard est **le mari** de Paule.
1407   husband

la hutte
1408   hut

le buffet
1409   hutch/sideboard*

la jacinthe
1410   hyacinth

La chorale chante **un hymne**.
1411   hymn

un trait d'union
«Après-midi» prend un trait d'union.
There is a hyphen in ''après-midi''.
1412   hyphen

La glace flotte dans le verre.

1413 ice

la glace, la crème glacée

1414 ice cream

Un iceberg peut faire couler un bateau.

1415 iceberg

De longs **glaçons** pendent du toit.

1416 icicle

le glaçage du gâteau

1417 icing

Elle vient d'avoir **une idée**!

1418 idea

des jumelles **identiques**

1419 identical twins

idiot

1420 idiot

oisif

1421 idle

si

Si j'avais un marteau, je ne m'en servirais que quand personne ne dort.

If I had a hammer, I would only hammer when no one was sleeping.

1422 if

un igloo

1423 igloo

la clé de contact

1424 ignition key

malade, souffrant

1425 ill

illuminer, éclairer

1426 to illuminate

une illustration

Dans un livre de contes, il y a des mots et **des illustrations**.

Storybooks have words and illustrations.

1427 illustration

important

Ce qui est **important** pour Julie n'est peut-être pas **important** pour Luc.
Savoir lire et écrire, c'est **important**.

What is important to Julie may not be important to Luc.
It is important to be able to read and write.

1428 important

en, dans

Nous faisons une promenade **en** forêt.
Nous avons pris des sandwichs **dans** notre sac.

We are going for a walk in the forest.
We have brought sandwiches in our bag.

1429 in

l'encens

1430 incense

Il y a douze **pouces** dans un pied.

1431 inch

un index

Il y a **un index** à la fin de ce livre.
L'index contient tous les mots de ce dictionnaire.

There is an index at the back of this book.
The index contains all the words in the dictionary.

1432   index

L'indigo est un bleu violet.

1433   indigo

Marie a décidé de rester **à l'intérieur**.

1434   indoors

le bébé, le nourrisson

1435   infant

Tante Sylvie a **une infection**.

1436   infection

contagieux, communicatif

Sa maladie est **contagieuse**.
Papa a un rire **communicatif**.

Her condition is infectious.
Dad has an infectious laugh.

1437   infectious

Anne **fait savoir** à Paule qu'elle déménage.

1438   to inform

L'ours **habite** une caverne.

1439   The bear **inhabits** a cave.

Quelles sont tes **initiales**?

1440   initials

une injection, la piqûre

1441   injection

la blessure au doigt

1442   injury

L'encre est dans l'encrier.

1443   ink

un insecte

1444   insect

dedans, à l'intérieur

1445   inside

J'**insiste** pour que tu prennes ton bain!

1446   to insist

inspecter, examiner

1447   to inspect

Sers-toi d'une cuillère **au lieu** d'une fourchette!

1449   Use a spoon **instead** of a fork!

des instructions

1450   instruction

un instructeur

1451   instructor

un inspecteur

1448   inspector

une isolation

Il y a de l'isolation dans les murs de la maison.
Il y a de l'isolation autour des fils électriques pour que les gens ne s'électrocutent pas.

There is insulation in the walls of the house.
There is insulation around the wires so people will not get a shock.

1452 insulation

le carrefour, une intersection

1453 intersection/crossroads*

une entrevue

1454 interview

Daniel entre **dans** la pièce.

1455 **into** the room

Maman **présente** Jérôme à Jerémie.

1456 to introduce

Les Vikings **envahissent** le village.

1457 to invade

La guerre a fait **des invalides**!

1458 invalid

Qu'est-ce qu'il a **inventé** là?!

1459 to invent

un homme **invisible**

1460 invisible

Quel plaisir de recevoir **une invitation**!

1461 invitation

Il l'**invite**.

1462 He is **inviting** her.

un iris

1463 iris

Julien **repasse** ses vêtements.

1464 to iron

le fer à repasser

1465 iron

le masque de **fer**

1466 iron mask

une île

1467 island

la démangeaison

Marc a des **démangeaisons** causées par l'herbe à puce.
S'il arrête de se gratter, **la démangeaison** partira.

Marc got a bad itch from poison ivy.
The itch will go away if he stops scratching.

1468 itch

démanger

1469 to itch

La peau me **démange**.

1470 My skin is **itchy**.

Le lierre pousse sur les murs.

1471 ivy

	donner un coup	Est-ce que **la veste** est à sa taille?	**la jaquette** du livre
	1472 to jab	1473 jacket	1474 dust jacket

un bord **dentelé**	derrière les barreaux de **la prison**	**la confiture**	**coincer, bloquer**
1475 jagged edge	1476 jail/gaol*	1477 jam	1478 to jam

Janvier est le premier mois de l'année.	**le bocal, la jarre**	**la mâchoire** du requin	**le jeans**
1479 January	1480 jar	1481 jaw	1482 jeans

la jeep	**la gelée**	le moteur **à réaction**	un avion **à réaction**
1483 jeep	1484 jelly	1485 jet engine	1486 jet plane

le bijou, le joyau	**le casse-tête, le puzzle**	faire **un travail**	**le jet d'eau**
1488 jewel	1489 jigsaw puzzle	1490 doing a job	1487 jet of water

Le jockey monte un cheval de course.

1491   jockey

faire du jogging, courir

1492   to jog

joindre les deux bouts

1493   to join

le joint, l'articulation

1494   joint

Monsieur Croûton rit de sa mauvaise **blague**.

1495   joke

Le juge décidera.

1496   judge

le jongleur

1497   juggler

Annie aime **le jus** d'orange frais.

1498   juice

Juillet est le septième mois de l'année.

1499   July

La grenouille **saute**.

1500   to jump

Elle **saute dans** la mare.

1501   to jump in

Elle **saute sur** un rocher.

1502   to jump on

Gilles est **un** excellent **sauteur**.

1503   jumper

une barboteuse

1504   jumper/pinafore*

les câbles de démarrage

1505   jumper cables/jump leads*

Juin est le sixième mois de l'année.

1506   June

Il y a des tigres dans **la jungle**.

1507   jungle

La jonque est un voilier chinois.

1508   junk

les déchets, la camelote

1509   junk

juste

Juste un peu, merci.
Le juge est juste.

Just a little, thanks.
The judge is a just person.

1510   just

le kaléidoscope

1511   kaleidoscope

Le petit **kangourou** est dans la poche de sa mère.

1512   kangaroo

la quille du bateau

1513   keel

Milou aime sa **niche**.

1514   kennel

le grain, la graine

1515   kernel

la bouilloire

1516   kettle

la clé, la clef

1517   key

donner un coup de pied

1518   to kick

un enfant

1519   kid

Le chevreau est le petit de la chèvre.

1520   kid

enlever, kidnapper

1521   to kidnap

le rein

1522   kidney

Le chasseur **a tué** le lion.

1523   to kill

le four du potier

1524   kiln

1 **kilogramme** = 1000 grammes

1525   kilogram

1 **kilomètre** = 1000 mètres

1526   kilometer/kilometre*

En Écosse, les hommes portent **le kilt**.

1527   kilt

La robe est **une sorte** de vêtement.

1528   A dress is a **kind** of garment.

une **gentille** petite fille

1529   **kind** girl

Le roi porte une couronne.

1530 king

le martin-pêcheur

1531 kingfisher

le kiosque à journaux

1532 kiosk

le hareng doux

1533 kippers

embrasser

1534 to kiss

Fais-moi **un baiser**.

1535 kiss

la cuisine

1536 kitchen

Le cerf-volant fait des pirouettes dans le ciel.

1537 kite

le chaton

1538 kitten

Le kiwi est un fruit savoureux.

1539 kiwi

le genou

1540 knee

se mettre à genoux, s'agenouiller

1541 to kneel

le couteau

1542 knife

Est-ce que tu sais **tricoter**?

1543 to knit

le bouton de porte

1544 knob

Frappe à la porte avant d'entrer!

1545 to knock

le nœud

1546 knot

savoir, connaître

Sais-tu ce que cela veut dire?
Je ne vous **connais** pas!

Do you know what this means?
I don't know you.

1547 to know

une articulation

1548 knuckle

Les koalas vivent en Australie.

1549 koala bear

L

L'**étiquette** prévient du danger.

1550   label

le laboratoire

1551   laboratory

un col de **dentelle**

1552   lace

un escabeau, une échelle

1554   ladder

la louche à soupe

1555   ladle

la dame

1556   lady

Marc **lace** ses souliers.

1553   to **lace**

la coccinelle

1557   ladybug/ladybird*

les biscuits à la cuiller,
les langues de chat

1558   ladyfingers

Le monstre est dans son
repaire.

1559   lair

Le lac est au milieu des terres.

1560   lake

un agneau

1561   lamb

Le pauvre âne est **estropié**.

1562   lame

la lampe

1563   lamp

le réverbère

1564   lamp-post

la lance du chevalier

1565   lance

la terre

1566   land

L'avion **atterrit**.

1567   to land

le palier

1568   landing

le propriétaire

Monsieur Carpin paie le loyer à son **propriétaire**.
La maison appartient à son **propriétaire**.

Mr. Carpin pays rent to his landlord.
The house belongs to the landlord.

1569   landlord

Les autoroutes ont plusieurs **voies**.

1570   lane

---

la langue

Combien de **langues** parles-tu?
Le français est **la langue** maternelle de Julie.

How many languages do you speak?
French is Julie's first language.

1571   language

---

la lanterne

1572   lantern

Elle tient le bébé sur ses **genoux**.

1573   lap

---

le mélèze

1574   larch

Le lard fond dans la poêle.

1575   lard

---

grand

1576   large

---

une alouette

1577   lark

---

le cil

1578   lash

---

le **dernier** morceau de gâteau

1579   the **last** piece

Certaines choses **durent** vraiment.

1580   Some things do **last**.

---

fermer au loquet

1581   to **latch**

Tu es en retard!

1582   You are **late**.

---

la mousse de savon

1583   lather

---

rire

1584   to laugh

La chaloupe les emmène au rivage.

1585   launch

---

lancer une fusée

1586   to **launch**

---

la plate-forme de lancement

1587   launchpad

---

le linge sale

1588   laundry/washing*

Carole fait sa lessive à **la laverie**.

1589   laundry/launderette*

La lavande sent bon.

1590   lavender

Obéis à **la loi**!

1591   Obey the law!

Qui a tondu **la pelouse**?

1592   lawn

poser des carreaux

1594   to **lay** tiles

des couches superposées

1595   **layer** upon **layer**

Il est **paresseux**.

1596   He is **lazy**.

la tondeuse à gazon

1593   lawn mower

Vincent **mène** le cheval.

1597   to **lead**

le chef, le guide

1598   leader

la feuille

1599   leaf

Le seau **fuit**.

1600   to **leak**

La Tour de Pise **penche**.

1601   to **lean**

J'apprends à lire.

1602   I **learn** to read.

la laisse de Fido

1603   leash/lead*

Les chaussures sont en **cuir**.

1604   Shoes are made of **leather**.

Je **laisse** ce paquet ici.

1605   to **leave**

partir, quitter

1606   to **leave**

le rebord de la fenêtre

1607   **ledge** of a window

le poireau

1608   leek

Tourne à **gauche**!	Il est **gaucher**.	**la jambe**	**la légende** du cyclope
1609 left	1610 He is left-handed.	1611 leg	1612 legend
le citron	**la limonade**	Je te **prête** ce livre.	**la lentille**, le verre de lunettes
1613 lemon	1614 lemonade	1615 to lend	1616 lens
Le léopard est à l'affût.	**le collant**	Il y en a **moins** ici.	**la leçon**
1617 leopard	1618 leotard	1619 There is **less** here.	1620 lesson
Lâche-moi!	**la lettre** de l'alphabet	Julie a écrit **une lettre**.	**La laitue** pousse au jardin.
1621 **Let** me go!	1622 letter of the alphabet	1623 letter	1624 lettuce
le niveau	**le levier**	**Le menteur** a été puni.	Silence à **la bibliothèque**!
1625 level surface	1626 lever	1627 liar	1628 library

la plaque d'immatriculation

1629   licence plate/number plate*

lécher

1630   to lick

le couvercle du pot

1631   lid

Pinocchio est en train de **mentir**.

1632   to lie

La vie de ce bébé vient de commencer.

1634   life

le canot de sauvetage

1635   lifeboat

lever, soulever

1636   to lift

se coucher

1633   to lie down

la lumière de la lampe

1637   light/table lamp*

Papa **allume** la bougie.

1638   to light

une ampoule

1639   lightbulb

Elle **allège** la charge.

1640   She **lightens** the load.

le phare

1641   lighthouse

la foudre, un éclair

1642   lightning

le paratonnerre

1643   lightning rod

Cora **aime** bien son chat.

1644   to like

probablement, vraisemblable

Sophie ne viendra **probablement** pas demain. C'est une explication **vraisemblable**.

Sophie is not likely to come tomorrow. That is a likely explanation.

1645   likely

Le lilas fleurit au printemps.

1646   lilac

le lis

1647   lily

la branche de l'arbre

1648   limb

la lime, le citron vert

1649   lime

la limite

La limite de vitesse est de 30 milles à l'heure.
La bonté de Mamie n'a pas de **limite**.

The speed limit is 30 miles per hour.
There is no limit to. Mamie's kindness.

1650   limit

Notre voisin **boite**.

1651   to **limp**

la ligne

Peux-tu dessiner **une ligne** vraiment droite?

1652   line

Le linge est empilé dans l'armoire.

1653   linen

Le paquebot vogue sur l'océan.

1654   liner

la doublure de la jaquette

1655   lining

unir, lier

1656   to **link**

la charpie

1657   lint

le lion

1658   lion

les lèvres

1659   lips

le rouge à lèvres

1660   lipstick

L'eau et le lait sont **des liquides**.

1661   liquid

la liste

1662   list

Ils **écoutent**.

1663   They are **listening**.

le litre

1664   liter/litre*

Il ne faut pas **jeter ses déchets**!

1665   to **litter**

une **petite** pomme

1666   a **little** apple

vivre

Julie **vit** à la ville.
Il serait difficile de **vivre** sur la lune.

Julie lives in the city.
It would be difficult to live on the moon.

1667   to **live**

animé

1668   lively

le salon

1669   living room/lounge*

le lézard

1670   lizard

Le soldat **charge** le canon.

1671   to load

charger un camion

1672   to load

la miche de pain

1673   loaf

prêter

Sébastien **a prêté** de l'argent à Julie parce qu'elle avait dépensé tout son argent de poche.

Sébastien loaned/lent Julie some money because she had spent her allowance.*

1674   to loan/lend*

un homard

1675   lobster

fermer à clé, verrouiller

1676   to lock

la locomotive

1678   locomotive

le criquet, la sauterelle

1679   locust

le chalet de ski

1680   lodge/chalet*

la serrure de la porte

1677   lock

Le grenier est sous le toit.

1681   loft

la bûche de bois

1682   log

Laura lèche **la sucette**.

1683   lollipop

seul, solitaire

1684   lonely

La girafe a un cou très **long**.

1685   long

Lucien **regarde** par la fenêtre.

1686   to look

le métier à tisser

1687   loom

la boucle

1688   loop

Le bracelet est trop lâche.

1689   loose

Gérard **a perdu** une moufle.

1690   to lose

la lotion pour la peau

1691   lotion

La musique est trop **bruyante.**

1692   loud

le haut-parleur

1693   loudspeaker

s'étendre paresseusement

1694   to lounge

l'amour

L'amour est une chose très importante.
Julie pense que quand on a de l'amour, on a tout dans la vie.

*Love is very important.
Julie thinks that if you have love you have everything.*

1695   love

Ils s'aiment.

1696   to love

belle, jolie

1697   lovely

la branche **basse**

1698   low branch

baisser, abaisser

1699   to lower

chanceux

Martin est **chanceux** de visiter la Suisse.
Julie est **chanceuse** d'avoir un si gentil petit frère.

*Martin is lucky to be able to visit Switzerland.
Julie is lucky to have such a cute little brother.*

1700   lucky

les bagages

1701   luggage

L'eau **tiède** n'est ni chaude, ni froide.

1702   lukewarm water

Maman chante **une berceuse.**

1703   lullaby

le bois de construction

1704   lumber/timber*

Il a **une** grosse **bosse.**

1705   lump

le déjeuner

1706   lunch

la boîte à lunch, à déjeuner

1707   lunchbox

le poumon

1708   lung

le magazine, la revue

1709　　magazine

Les asticots ne sont pas beaux.

1710　　maggot

La magie est parfois étrange.

1711　　magic

Un aimant attire les clous.

1713　　magnet

un lion **magnifique**

1714　　magnificent

La loupe grossit l'insecte.

1715　　magnifying glass

Le magicien fait apparaître un lapin.

1712　　magician

la pie

1716　　magpie

poster, envoyer par la poste

1717　　to mail/post*

Le facteur livre le courrier.

1718 mail carrier/postman*

Que **fait** Marc?

1719　　to make

le maquillage de Mélodie

1720　　makeup

le mâle et la femelle

1721　　male

le maillet

1722　　mallet

un homme

1723　　man

La mandarine est un fruit juteux.

1724　　mandarin

Il joue de **la mandoline**.

1725　　mandolin

la crinière du cheval

1726　　mane

La mangue est un fruit très sucré.

1727　　mango

Il a de bonnes **manières.**	**beaucoup**	**la carte** de géographie	Le sculpteur taille **le marbre.**
1728 He has good **manners.**	1729 many	1730 map	1731 marble
marcher	**Mars** est le troisième mois de l'année.	**La jument** est la femelle du cheval.	**les billes**
1733 to **march**	1734 **March**	1735 **mare**	1732 **marbles**
le souci, un œillet d'Inde	**marquer** la réponse correcte	Tu as eu de bonnes **notes.**	**le marché** de fruits et légumes
1736 **marigold**	1737 to **mark**	1738 **mark**	1739 **market**
se marier	**le marais**	faire de la purée, écraser les pommes de terre	**le masque**
1740 to **marry**	1741 **marsh**	1742 to **mash** potatoes	1743 **mask**
Une masse a un poids.	**le mât** du voilier	Andrée **sait parfaitement faire** du vélo.	**le match, la partie** de tennis
1744 **mass**	1745 **mast**	1746 to **master**	1747 **match**

Il ne faut pas jouer avec **les allumettes**!

1748   match

les mathématiques

$$2$$
$$+2$$
$$\overline{4}$$

1749   mathematics

une affaire

Tricher à l'école, c'est **une affaire** grave.
Le cerveau contient de **la matière** grise.

To cheat in school is a serious matter.
The brain contains grey matter.

1750   matter

Le matelas est vieux.

1751   mattress

Mai est le cinquième mois de l'année.

1752   May

peut-être

Julie devrait **peut-être** rester à la maison.
La réponse n'est ni oui, ni non : c'est **peut-être**.

Maybe Julie should stay home.
The answer is not yes, and it is not no, it is maybe.

1753   maybe

le maire de la ville

1754   mayor

Ne te perds pas dans **le labyrinthe**!

1755   maze

le pré, la prairie

1756   meadow

la grande sturnelle

1757   meadowlark

le repas

1758   meal

un **méchant** garçon

1759   mean person

Francine a **la rougeole**.

1760   measles

La règle sert à **mesurer** la longueur.

1 2 3 4 5 6

1761   to measure

la viande

1762   meat

le mécanicien

1763   mechanic

la médaille d'honneur

1764   medal

Le médecin prescrit **des médicaments**.

1765   medicine

moyen

1766   medium

rencontrer

1767   to **meet**

la réunion des professeurs

1768 meeting

le melon

1769 melon

Le glaçon fond.

1770 to melt

Notre club a quatre **membres**.

1771 Our club has four **members**.

le menu du restaurant

1772 menu

la merci, la pitié

Nous sommes à **la merci** du temps.
Les bandits n'ont eu aucune **pitié**.

We are at the mercy of the weather.
The bandits showed no mercy to anyone.

1773 mercy

la sirène

1774 mermaid

gai, joyeux

1775 merry

un désordre terrible

1776 a real mess

Voilà **un message** pour toi.

1777 message

la messagère

1778 messenger

La chope est en **métal**.

1779 metal

Les météorites tombent du ciel.

1780 meteorite

le compteur

1781 meter

le mètre

1782 meter/metre*

la méthode

Julie a **une méthode** pour apprendre vite.
Une méthode, c'est une manière de faire les choses.

Julie has a method to learn quickly.
A method is a way of doing things.

1783 method

le métronome

1784 metronome

le microphone, le micro

1785 microphone

le microscope

1786 microscope

le four à micro-ondes

1787 microwave oven

midi	**au milieu**
1788 midday	1789 in the middle
le nain	**minuit**
1790 midget	1791 midnight

le mille

Un mille a 5280 pieds.
La vitesse limite est de 30 **milles** à l'heure.

*One mile has 5280 feet.
The speed limit is 30 miles
per hour.*

1792   mile

le lait de la vache

1793   milk

Le moulin est au bord
de la rivière.

1794   mill

l'esprit, l'intelligence

E=MC²

1795   mind

La mine est sous la terre.

1796   mine

Ce **mineur** qui travaille
dans la mine examine la roche.

1797   miner

les minéraux

1798   minerals

le vairon, le méné

1799   minnow

Ces bonbons ont le goût de
la menthe.

1800   mint

moins

7 − 5 = 2

1801   minus

Il y a soixante **minutes**
dans une heure.

1802   minute

un drôle de **miracle**

1803   miracle

le mirage dans le désert

1804   mirage

le miroir

1805   mirror

L'avare aime ses sous.

1806   miser

Ma famille me **manque**.

1807   to miss

le missile

1808   missile

Michel s'est perdu dans **le brouillard**.

1809   mist

le gui

1810   mistletoe

le gant, la moufle

1811   mittens

mélanger

1812   to mix

le mélangeur, le mixeur

1813   mixer

le fossé, les douves

1814   moat

L'oiseau **se moque** du chat.

1815   to mock

un oiseau moqueur

1816   mockingbird

la maquette d'avion

1817   model airplane/aeroplane*

une chaise **moderne**

1818   modern chair

Sa couche est **humide**.

1819   moist

la taupe

1820   mole

le grain de beauté

1821   mole

Un moment s'il te plaît!

1822   One **moment** please.

lundi

Lundi est le premier jour de la semaine pour les écoliers.

Monday is the first day of the school week.

1823   Monday

l'argent

1824   money

le singe

1825   monkey

la lotte, l'ange de mer

1826   monkfish

Quel horrible **monstre**!

1827   monster

Il y a 12 **mois** dans l'année.

1828　　month

le monument

1829　　monument

Il est de bonne **humeur**.

1830　He is in a good **mood**.

Il est de mauvaise **humeur**.

1831　He is in a bad **mood**.

un croissant de **lune**

1832　　moon

un orignal

1833　　moose

le matin

1834　　morning

le mortier et le pilon

1835　mortar and pestle

la mosaïque

1836　　mosaic

Le moustique pique.

1837　　mosquito

La mousse pousse sur les arbres.

1838　　moss

la mère, la maman

1839　　mother

le moteur

1840　　motor

la motocyclette

1841　　motorcycle

le moule à gâteaux

1842　mould*/mold

la motte, la butte

1843　　mound

se mettre en selle, monter

1844　to mount

la montagne

1845　　mountain

la souris

1846　　mouse

Jules a **une** grosse **moustache**.

1847　moustache*/mustache

la bouche

1848   mouth

L'escargot **bouge** lentement.

1849   to move

le mouvement du balancier

1850   movement

le film

1851   movie/film*

tondre la pelouse

1852   to **mow** the lawn

C'est **trop** pour moi.

1853   too **much** for me

Pourquoi s'est-il assis dans **la boue**?

1854   mud

la mule

1855   mule

multiplier

1856   multiply

Maurice a **les oreillons**.

1857   mumps

Assassiner quelqu'un, c'est un crime horrible.

1858   to murder

le muscle

1859   muscle

Le musée contient des choses rares.

1860   museum

Certains **champignons** sont vénéneux.

1861   mushroom

Julie aime **la musique**.

1862   music

La maman de Julie est **musicienne**.

1863   musician

Les moules vivent sur les rochers dans la mer.

1864   mussel

Tu **dois** sauter!

1865   You **must** jump.

la moutarde

1866   mustard

Il a **une muselière** sur **le museau**.

1867   muzzle

N

le clou

1868　　nail

un ongle

1869　　finger**nail**

**la pince à ongles,
le coupe-ongles**

1870　　**nail** clipper

Ils sont tous les deux **nus**.

1872　　naked

Mon **nom** est…

1873　　My **name** is…

la serviette

1874　　napkin/serviette*

clouer

1871　　to **nail**

trop **étroit** pour passer

1875　　too **narrow** to pass

Certaines **nations**
sont des îles.

1876　　nation

naturel

Les aliments **naturels** sont
bons à la santé.
Les fruits contiennent
du sucre **naturel**.

*It is healthy to eat natural
foods.
Fruit contains natural sugar.*

1877　　natural

La nature est belle.

1878　　nature

Elle est **méchante**.

1879　　She is **naughty**.

La capitaine **navigue** à
l'étoile.

1880　　to **navigate**

Elle est tout **près** du but.

1881　　near

net, propre

1882　　neat

pas agréable, mais **nécessaire**

1883 Not pleasant, but necessary.

le cou

1884　　neck

le collier

1885　　necklace

L'abeille fait du miel avec
le nectar.

1886　　nectar

la nectarine, le brugnon

1887   nectarine

le besoin

Julie aide toujours ses amis quand ils sont dans **le besoin**.
Se loger et manger sont **des besoins** fondamentaux.

Julie always helps her friends in need.
Food and shelter are basic human needs.

1888   need

J'ai besoin d'eau.

1889   I **need** water.

Tu sais enfiler une aiguille?

1890   needle

Il néglige son chien.

1891   He **neglects** his dog.

Le cheval hennit.

1892   to neigh

les voisins

1893 neighbors/neighbours*

Ni l'une ni l'autre ne me va.

1894   **neither** one fits

une enseigne au néon

1895   neon sign

Mon neveu est le fils de mon frère.

1896 My **nephew** is my brother's son.

le nerf

1897   nerve

Robert est nerveux.

1898   nervous

deux œufs dans le nid

1899   nest

Les orties piquent.

1900   nettle

Ne joue jamais avec le feu!

1901   **Never** play with fire!

un chapeau neuf

1902   new

les nouvelles

Maman lit les **nouvelles**.
J'ai de bonnes **nouvelles** pour toi!

Mother reads the news.
I have good news for you!

1903   news

le journal

1904   newspaper

Au suivant!

1905   Next !

grignoter, ronger

1906   to nibble

L'un des deux est **gentil**.

1907   nice

le nickel

1908   nickel

le surnom

Son prénom est Ariane, mais son **surnom** est Nanou.

Her name is Ariane, but her nickname is Nanou.

1909   nickname

Ma **nièce** est la fille de mon frère.

1910 My **niece** is my brother's daughter.

Les hiboux chassent **la nuit**.

1911   night

le rossignol

1912   nightingale

Bastien fait **un cauchemar**.

1913   nightmare

neuf

1914   nine

La réponse est **non**.

1916   no

noble

Sir Du Val est **noble** et généreux. Aider une vieille dame à traverser la rue est une action **noble**.

Sir Du Val is noble and generous. Helping an old lady across the street is a noble deed.

1917   noble

le gentilhomme

1918   nobleman

le neuvième

1915   ninth

Il n'y a **personne** ici.

1919   nobody

le bruit

1920   noise

À **midi**, le soleil est au zénith.

1921   noon

le nord

1922   north

J'ai une mouche sur **le nez**!

1923   nose

la noix

1924   nuts

le casse-noix

1925   nutcracker

les bas de **nylon**

1926 nylon stockings/tights*

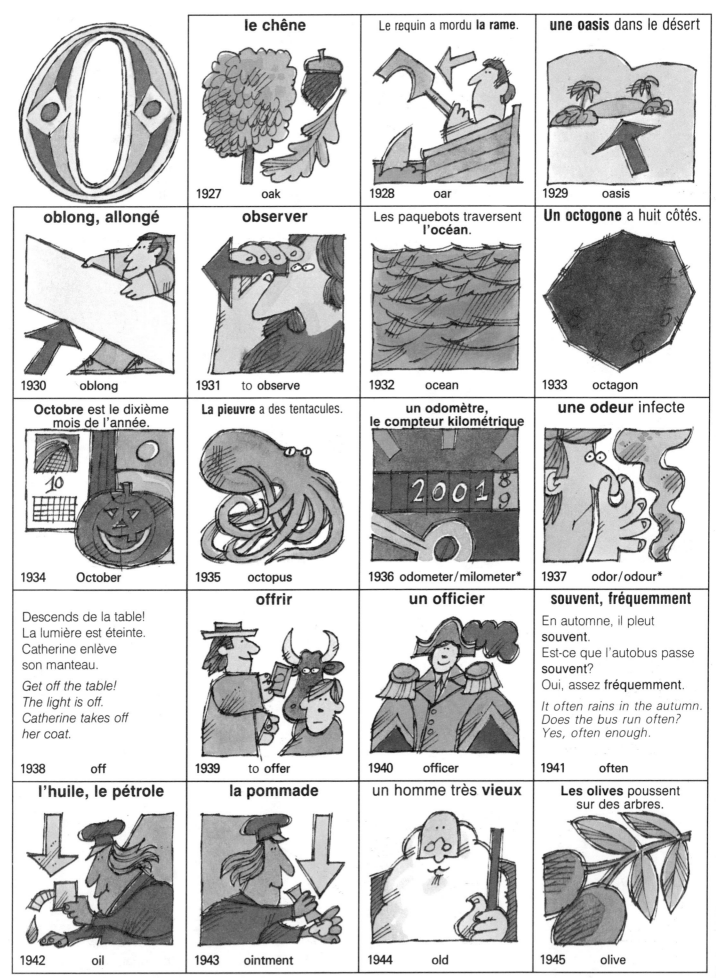

le chêne

1927   oak

Le requin a mordu **la rame**.

1928   oar

une oasis dans le désert

1929   oasis

oblong, allongé

1930   oblong

observer

1931   to observe

Les paquebots traversent **l'océan**.

1932   ocean

Un octogone a huit côtés.

1933   octagon

Octobre est le dixième mois de l'année.

1934   October

La pieuvre a des tentacules.

1935   octopus

un odomètre, le compteur kilométrique

1936   odometer/milometer*

une odeur infecte

1937   odor/odour*

Descends de la table!
La lumière est éteinte.
Catherine enlève
son manteau.

*Get off the table!
The light is off.
Catherine takes off
her coat.*

1938   off

offrir

1939   to offer

un officier

1940   officer

souvent, fréquemment

En automne, il pleut
souvent.
Est-ce que l'autobus passe
souvent?
Oui, assez **fréquemment**.

*It often rains in the autumn.
Does the bus run often?
Yes, often enough.*

1941   often

l'huile, le pétrole

1942   oil

la pommade

1943   ointment

un homme très **vieux**

1944   old

Les olives poussent sur des arbres.

1945   olive

Le cuisinier fait **une omelette**.

1946   omelette

Le pot de fleurs est **sur** la table.

1947   **on** the table

une fois

Il était **une fois** une petite fille appelée Julie...
Guillaume a voyagé en Chine **une** seule **fois**.

*Once upon a time, there was a little girl called Julie...
Guillaume has travelled only once to China.*

1948   once

le chiffre **un**

1949   one

un oignon

1950   onion

mon **seul** amour

1951   my **only** love

Ne laisse pas la porte **ouverte**!

1952   open

ouvrir

1953   to **open**

Jacques se sentira mieux après **l'opération**.

1954   operation

un opossum

1955   opossum

contraire, en face

Le bien est **le contraire** du mal.
La famille Gervais vit **en face** de chez nous.

*Good is the opposite of bad.
The Gervais family lives opposite us.*

1956   opposite

ou

Tu peux faire tes devoirs **ou** nettoyer ta chambre.
Préfères-tu une poire **ou** une pomme?

*You can do your homework or tidy up your room.
Do you prefer a pear or an apple?*

1957   or

Il faut peler **une orange**.

1958   orange

la couleur **orange**

1959   orange

Le verger est plein d'arbres fruitiers.

1960   orchard

un orchestre

1961   orchestra

une orchidée

1962   orchid

Édouard **commande** un repas.

1963   to **order**

l'origan, la marjolaine

1964   oregano

Albert joue de **l'orgue**.

1965   organ

le loriot

1966   oriole

Un orphelin n'a pas de parents.

1967   orphan

Une autruche ne peut pas voler.

1968   ostrich

La loutre aime manger du poisson.

1969   otter

Il y a seize **onces** dans une livre.

1970   ounce

---

dehors, à l'extérieur

1971   outdoors

Tu aimes ma **tenue**?

1972   outfit

---

ovale

1973   oval

Il y a une tarte dans **le four.**

1974   oven

Un homme **à la mer!**

1975   Man overboard!

---

le pardessus

1976   overcoat

Le seau **déborde**.

1977   to overflow

---

la galoche

1978   overshoe

---

chavirer, se renverser

1979   to overturn

---

devoir

Mieux vaut ne pas **devoir** d'argent.
Tu **dois** le respect à ton professeur.

It is best not to owe any money.
You owe respect to your teacher.

1980   to owe

---

le hibou, la chouette

1981   owl

---

posséder, avoir

Nous **possédons** la maison où nous habitons.
Julie a 2 paires de chaussures.

We own the house we live in.
Julie owns 2 pairs of shoes.

1982   to own

---

le bœuf

1983   ox

Le plongeur a besoin d'**oxygène**.

1984   oxygen

Cette **huître** contient une perle.

1985   oyster

P

Julie **fait ses bagages**.
1986   to pack

le colis
1987   package

le bloc
1988   pad

Isabelle tient **la pagaie**.
1990   paddle

pagayer
1991   to paddle

le cadenas
1992   padlock

la plate-forme de lancement
1989   pad

Tourne **la page**!
1993   page

Le seau d'eau est lourd.
1994   pail

la peinture
1996   paint

Ne touche pas **la peinture** fraîche!
1997   wet paint

la douleur
1995   pain

le peintre
2000   painter

Bastien **peint** la barrière.
1998   to paint

le pinceau
1999   paintbrush

la peinture
2001   painting

une paire de chaussures
2002   a pair of shoes

le palais
2003   palace

Cette fleur est de couleur **pâle**.
2004   pale

la palette du peintre

2005   palette

la paume de la main

2006   palm

la casserole

2007   pan

Julie raffole **des crêpes**.

2008   pancake

le panda

2009   panda

la console

2010   panel

Fabrice joue de **la flûte de Pan**.

2011   panpipe

la pensée

2012   pansy

Blanchot **halète**.

2013   to pant

la panthère

2014   panther

le pantalon

2015   pants/trousers*

La papaye est
un fruit comestible.

2016   papaya

le papier

2017   paper

Le parachute freine sa chute.

2018   parachute

la parade, **le défilé**

2019   parade

des lignes **parallèles**

2020   parallel lines

figé par la peur,
paralysé par la peur

2021   paralyzed/paralysed*

Julie a reçu **un colis**.

2022   parcel

Le père et la mère sont
les parents.

2023   parent

Grand-mère est
dans **le parc**.

2024   park

garer, stationner

2025   to park

la parka

2026   parka

le parlement

2027   parliament

Le perroquet répète tout ce que je dis.

2028   parrot

le persil

2029   parsley

Le panais est un légume comestible.

2030   parsnip

Il y a **des particules** de poussière dans l'air.

2031   particle

le partenaire

2032   partner

la fête, la soirée

2033   party

Marie **passe** la balle...

2034   to pass

et Henri **tombe dans les pommes** sous le choc.

2035   to pass out

le passage

2036   passage

La passagère ne rame pas.

2037   passenger

Il faut **un passeport** pour aller à l'étranger.

2038   passport

passé

Dans **le passé**, il n'y avait ni avions ni autos.
Hier, c'est **le passé**; demain, c'est l'avenir.

In the past, there were no planes or cars. Yesterday is the past, tomorrow is the future.

2039   past

les pâtes, les nouilles

2040   pasta

Émile **colle** du papier peint.

2041   to paste

La broderie est **le passe-temps** favori de Marie.

2042   pastime

la pâtisserie

2043   pastry

le pré, le pâturage

2044   pasture

une pièce bien nécessaire

2045   patch

le chemin, le sentier

2046   path

Elle est **patiente**.

2047   She is patient.

Le patient semble inquiet.

2048   patient

le patron de couture

2049   pattern

**faire une pause,
s'arrêter un instant**

Après deux pages de
lecture, Julie a fait une
pause.
Il faut que je m'arrête un
instant pour reprendre
mon souffle.

*After reading two pages,
Julie paused.
I have to pause for breath.*

2050   to pause

marcher sur **la chaussée**

2051   pavement/road*

Combien de **pattes** a-t-il?

2052   paw

payer avec des pièces
et des billets

2053   to pay

le téléphone **payant**

2054 pay phone/phone box*

Paix sur la terre!

2055   peace

La pêche a un noyau.

2056   peach

Le paon fait la roue.

2057   peacock

le pic, le sommet

2058   peak

le son de la cloche

2059   peal of a bell

une arachide, la cacahouète

2060   peanut

la poire

2061   pear

La perle est logée dans l'huître.

2062   pearl

Les pois sont dans la cosse.

2063   peas

la tourbe pour les plantes

2064   peat moss

le caillou, le galet

2065   pebbles

la pacane

2066   pecan

picorer du bec

2067   to peck

la pédale du vélo

2068   pedal

Le piéton marche sur le trottoir.

2070   pedestrian

le passage pour piétons

2071   pedestrian crossing

peler, éplucher

2072   to peel

Mélanie **pédale** fort.

2069   to pedal

Le pélican a un bec très long.

2073   pelican

le stylo

2074   pen

le crayon

2075   pencil

Le pendule oscille.

2076   pendulum

le pingouin

2077   penguin

le canif

2078   penknife

Le pentagone a cinq côtés.

2079   pentagon

les gens, le peuple

2080   people

Les graines de **poivre** sont à côté du poivrier.

2081   pepper

la menthe poivrée

2082   peppermint

la perche

2083   perch

L'oiseau a trouvé **un perchoir**.

2084   perch

un spectacle très réussi
2085   performance

le parfum
2086   perfume

On met **un point** en fin de phrase.
2087   period/full stop*

La pervenche a des pétales bleus.
2088   periwinkle

la personne
2089   person

un insecte nuisible
2090   pest

Gaétan **embête** son papa.
2091   to pester

un animal familier
2092   pet

Combien de **pétales** a cette fleur?
2094   petal

le pétunia
2095   petunia

La pharmacienne vend des médicaments.
2096   pharmacist/chemist*

caresser, câliner
2093   to pet

la pharmacie
2097   pharmacy/chemist's*

le faisan
2098   pheasant

le téléphone
2099   phone

la photographie, la photo
2100   photograph

le piano de la maman de Julie
2101   piano

Choisis une carte!
2102   to pick

lever, soulever
2103   to pick up

la pioche
2104   pickaxe

les cornichons

2105   pickles

faire des conserves au vinaigre

2106   to pickle

un pique-nique à la campagne

2107   picnic

Le tableau de Pablo est très moderne.

2108   picture

la tarte aux cerises

2109   pie

Mmmm! **un morceau** de tarte!

2110   a piece/slice* of pie

Mélanie **joint** les deux morceaux de l'anse.

2111   to piece together

la jetée, la digue

2112   pier

le cochon, le porc

2113   pig

le pigeon

2114   pigeon

Le cochon est dans **la porcherie**.

2115   pigsty

le tas, le monceau

2116   pile

le comprimé, le cachet

2117   pill/tablet*

le pilier, la colonne

2118   pillar

Comme il fait bon dormir sur **un coussin** ou **un oreiller**!

2119   pillow

la taie d'oreiller

2120   pillowcase

le pilote de l'avion

2121   pilot

la verrue

2122   pimple

Le crabe a **des pinces**.

2123   pincers

Pincer fait mal.

2124   to pinch

le sapin

2125 pine

un ananas

2126 pineapple

la couleur **rose**

2127 pink

Maurice aime fumer **la pipe**.

2128 pipe

Le pirate est éclopé.

2129 pirate

la pistache

2130 pistachio

un pistolet ancien

2131 pistol

Georges **lance la balle**.

2132 to pitch

avoir pitié

Julie **a pitié** de Luc qui a perdu son chat.

Julie pities Luc, who lost his cat.

2136 to pity

un endroit, la place

Cet **endroit** est parfait pour un pique-nique.
Jean remet le marteau à sa **place**.

This place is perfect for a picnic.
Jean puts the hammer back in its place.

2137 place

le carrelet, la plie

2138 plaice

Bravo Georges, bien lancé!
Ce piano est mal accordé.

Hey Georges, that was a good pitch.
This piano is off pitch.

2133 pitch

Elle porte une chemise **unie**.

2139 **plain** shirt

La plaine s'étend sur des centaines de kilomètres.

2140 plain

L'architecte **fait des plans**.

2141 to plan

la fourche du fermier

2134 pitchfork

le rabot du menuisier

2142 plane

Les planètes tournent autour du soleil.

2143 planets

la planche

2144 plank

le goudron

2135 pitch tar

la plante — Le jardinier **plante** des fleurs.

2145　plants　　　2146　to plant

le plâtre — Elle **plâtre** le mur.

2147　plaster　　　2148　to plaster

Deux objets en **plastique**.

2149　plastic

la pâte à modeler

2150　plasticine

C'est **l'assiette** de Julie.

2151　plate

le plateau

2152　plateau

le quai de la gare

2153　platform

Ils **jouent** dans le bac à sable et dans **l'aire de jeux**.

2154　to play　　　2155　playground

les cartes à jouer

2156　playing cards

Il **supplie** le bourreau.

2157　to plead

une journée **agréable**

2158　a pleasant day

Un verre de lait, **s'il vous plaît**.

2159　A glass of milk, please.

le pli

2160　pleat

la pince, la tenaille

2161　pliers

Le fermier **laboure** son champ.

2162　plow/plough*

plumer une volaille

2163　to pluck

Branche le fil dans la prise!

2164　plug

Le fermier laboure son champ avec **la charrue**.

2165 plug

la prune

2166 plum

le plombier

2167 plumber

dodu, grassouillet

2168 plump

le pluriel

«Un» est singulier,
«deux ou plus» est **pluriel**.

''One is singular,
''two or more'' is plural.

2169 plural

Un **plus** un font...

2170 plus

le contreplaqué

2171 plywood

Jacques **fait pocher** des œufs.

2172 to poach

la poche

2173 pocket

la cosse du petit pois

2174 pea pod

le poème

Un poème est fait de vers qui riment.
Mais tous **les poèmes** ne sont pas sublimes.

*A poem has sets of lines which rhyme.
But not all poems are sublime.*

2175 poem

indiquer, montrer du doigt

2177 to point

la poinsettie

2176 poinsettia

le poison

2180 poison

vénéneux, vénimeux

Certains champignons sont **vénéneux**.
La plupart des serpents ne sont pas **vénimeux**.

*Some mushrooms are poisonous.
Most snakes are not poisonous.*

2181 poisonous

La pointe de la flèche est aiguë.

2178 point

pousser du doigt

2182 to poke

un ours **polaire**

2183 polar bear

le poteau

2184 pole

pointu

2179 pointed

le policier, l'agent de police	l'agente de police	polir, lisser	poli
			Ce n'est pas **poli** de crier. Le professeur attend une réponse **polie**. *It is not polite to shout. The teacher expects a polite answer.*
2185 policeman	2186 policewoman	2187 to polish	2188 polite

Julie est allergique au **pollen** des fleurs.	**La grenade** est un fruit.	**un étang** au milieu des bois	**le poney** de Joséphine
2189 pollen	2190 pomegranate	2191 pond	2192 pony

Ils nagent dans **la piscine**.	**mettre en commun**	pauvre, piètre	**faire sauter** le bouchon
		Sa famille n'est ni **pauvre**, ni riche. Julie a obtenu de **piètres** résultats parce qu'elle n'a pas travaillé dur. *Her family is not poor, but it is not rich either. Julie had poor results because she did not work hard.*	
2193 pool	2194 to pool	2195 poor	2196 to pop

le peuplier	le pavot, le coquelicot		le porche
		Beaucoup de gens aiment Julie. Ce livre plaît à beaucoup de gens. *Julie is a popular girl. This book is very popular.*	
2197 poplar	2198 poppy	2199 popular	2200 porch

Les pores sont des petits troùs de la peau.	le porridge, la bouillie	le port	portatif
			Julie veut une radio **portative**, mais elle n'a pas fait assez d'économies. *Julie wants a portable radio but she has not saved up enough money.*
2201 Pores are little holes in the skin.	2202 porridge	2203 port	2204 portable

le porteur	**le portrait** de tante Alice
2205 porter	2206 portrait

le poteau, le pilier	Pierre **poste** une lettre.
2207 post	2208 to post

la carte postale	**une affiche**
2210 postcard	2211 poster

le pot	**le bureau de poste**
2212 pot	2209 post office

la pomme de terre	**la poterie, la céramique**
2213 potato	2214 pottery

la bourse, le sac	**sauter, bondir**
2215 pouch	2216 to pounce

la livre	**frapper, taper**
Quatre bananes pèsent environ **une livre**.	
Four bananas weigh about a pound.	
2217 pound.	2218 to pound

verser	**bouder**
2219 to pour	2220 to pout

la poudre	**pratiquer, s'exercer**
2221 powder	2222 to practice/practise*

Le blé pousse dans **la prairie**.	**louer, glorifier**
2223 prairie	2224 to praise

Le cheval piaffe.

2225   to prance

prier

2226   to pray

Je préfère celle-là.

2227   to prefer

Elle est enceinte.

2228   She is pregnant.

Je suis présent.

2229   I am present.

le cadeau d'anniversaire

2230   birthday present

présenter, décerner un prix

2231   to present

les conserves de fruits

2232   preserved fruit

presser, appuyer

2233   to press

une jolie fillette

2234   pretty

La chouette a attrapé une proie.

2235   prey

Le prix est marqué sur l'étiquette.

2236   price

piquer

2237   to prick

un animal armé de piquants

2238   prickly animal

une école primaire

2239   primary school

la primevère à grandes fleurs

2240   primrose

le prince

2241   prince

la princesse

2242   princess

la directrice d'école

2243   school principal/Head teacher*

le principe

En **principe**, je suis d'accord avec toi.
Le premier **principe**, c'est de travailler dur.

In principle, I agree with you.
The first principle is to work hard.

2244   principle

imprimer

2245   to print

le prisme

2246   prism

Le voleur est allé en **prison**.

2247   prison

le prisonnier

2248   prisoner

privé

Julie et moi avons une conversation **privée**.
C'est une propriété **privée**.

Julie and I are having a private conversation.
This is private property.

2249   private

le prix, la récompense

2250   prize

le problème

2251   problem

les produits maraîchers

2252   produce

Il y a peu de bons **programmes** à la télévision.

2254   program / programme*

Interdit aux chiens!

2255   prohibited

le projet

Lucie est en train de travailler à **un projet** difficile.
Julie n'a pas bien réussi son **projet**.

Lucie is working on a difficult project.
Julie did not do well on her project.

2256   project

Cette usine **fabrique** des voitures.

2253   This factory **produces** cars.

Je promets.

2257   I promise.

la dent de la fourche

2258   prong

Prononce bien tes mots!

2259   to pronounce

la preuve de sa culpabilité

2260   proof of guilt

appuyer, soutenir

2261   to prop

une hélice

2262   propeller

correctement vêtu

2263   properly dressed

la propriété

Julie dit «C'est à moi» quand elle veut dire «C'est ma **propriété**».
Sa famille a **une propriété** à la campagne.

Julie says "This is mine" when she means "This is my property".
Her family owns property in the country.

2264   property

manifester, protester

2265   to protest

Je suis un chat **fier**.

2266   I am a **proud** cat.

Je peux le **prouver**!

2267   to prove

le proverbe

Voici **un proverbe** :
«Pierre qui roule n'amasse pas mousse.»

*Here is a proverb:
"A rolling stone gathers no moss."*

2268   proverb

fournir des chaises

2269   to **provide** chairs

Un pruneau est une prune séchée.

2270   prune

tailler, élaguer

2271   to prune

le téléphone **public**

2272   public telephone/phone box*

le pouding

2273   pudding/afters*

la flaque d'eau

2274   puddle

lancer des bouffées

2275   to puff

le macareux

2276   puffin

tirer

2277   to pull

la poulie

2278   pulley

le pull-over, le chandail

2279   pullover/sweater*

Le médecin lui prend **le pouls**.

2280   pulse

la pompe

2281   pump

Elle **pompe** de toutes ses forces.

2282   to pump

le potiron, la citrouille

2283   pumpkin

donner un coup de poing

2284   to punch

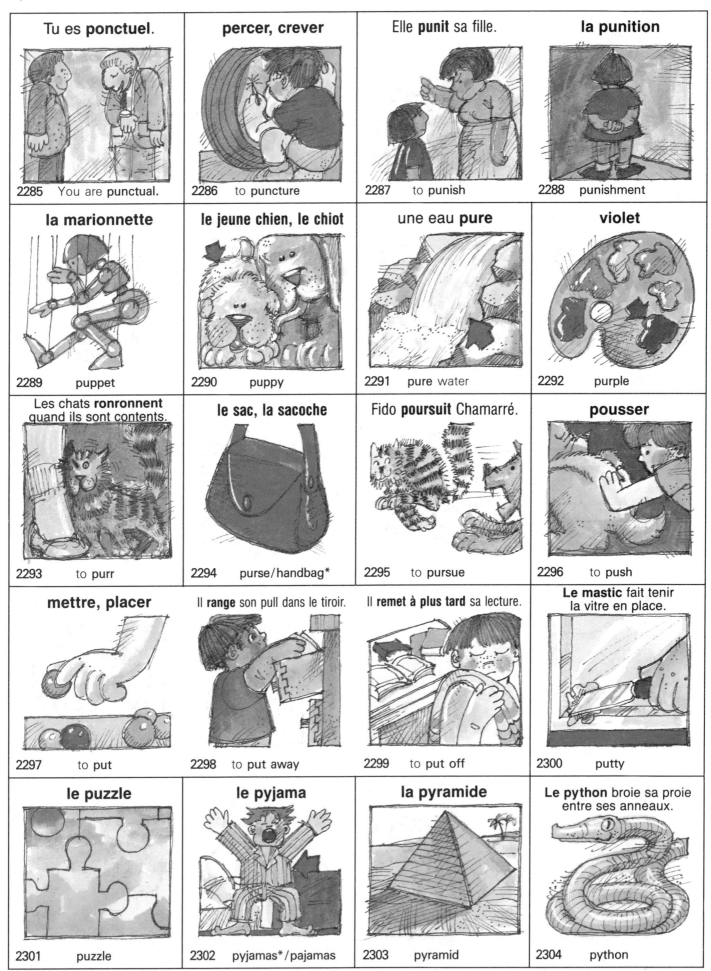

Tu es ponctuel.
2285 You are punctual.

percer, crever
2286 to puncture

Elle **punit** sa fille.
2287 to punish

la punition
2288 punishment

la marionnette
2289 puppet

le jeune chien, le chiot
2290 puppy

une eau **pure**
2291 pure water

violet
2292 purple

Les chats **ronronnent** quand ils sont contents.
2293 to purr

le sac, la sacoche
2294 purse/handbag*

Fido **poursuit** Chamarré.
2295 to pursue

pousser
2296 to push

mettre, placer
2297 to put

Il **range** son pull dans le tiroir.
2298 to put away

Il **remet à plus tard** sa lecture.
2299 to put off

Le mastic fait tenir la vitre en place.
2300 putty

le puzzle
2301 puzzle

le pyjama
2302 pyjamas*/pajamas

la pyramide
2303 pyramid

Le python broie sa proie entre ses anneaux.
2304 python

la caille

2305   quail

une montre de qualité

2306   quality watch

la quantité

2307   quantity

se disputer, se quereller

2308   to quarrel

Est-ce **une carrière** de pierres ou de sable?

2309   quarry

le quart

2310   quarter

Le bateau est amarré au **quai**.

2311   quay

la reine

2312   queen

poser **une question**

2313   to ask a question

rapide comme l'éclair

2314   quick

Il s'enfonce dans **les sables mouvants**.

2315   quicksand

Elle est **calme, tranquille**.

2316   She is quiet.

Autrefois, on écrivait à **la plume**.

2317   quill

les piquants du porc-épic

2318   porcupine quill

la couverture piquée

2319   quilt/eiderdown*

Le coing est un fruit âpre.

2320   quince

un carquois plein de flèches

2321   quiver

trembler, frissonner

2322   to quiver

le contrôle, la colle

Hier, nous avons eu **un contrôle** d'histoire.
Aujourd'hui, nous avons eu **une colle** en classe de géo.

Yesterday, we had a history quiz.
Today, we had a geography quiz.

2323   quiz

R

le lapin
2324   rabbit

le raton laveur
2325   raccoon

Le lièvre et la tortue **font la course**.
2326   to race

le porte-manteau
2327   rack/hat-stand*

le tapage, le vacarme
2328   racket

Le radiateur chauffe la pièce.
2329   radiator

la radio
2330   radio

le radis
2331   radish

le rayon du cercle
2332   radius

Le radeau descend au fil de l'eau.
2333   raft

Une attaque a lieu.
2334   a **raid** in progress

Tiens bien **la rampe**!
2335   handrail/banister*

la voie ferrée
2336   railroad track/railway track*

Il **pleut** des cordes!
2337   to rain

Après la pluie, vient **l'arc-en-ciel**.
2338   rainbow

un imperméable
2339   raincoat

lever, soulever

Tous ceux qui veulent du chocolat, **levez** la main!
Elle **a soulevé** une question intéressante.

Everyone who wants chocolate, raise your hand!
She has raised an interesting question.

2340   to **raise**

les raisins secs
2341   raisin

le rateau
2342   rake

frapper à la porte
2343   to rap/knock*

rapide
2344   rapid

rare
2345   rare

une **éruption** de boutons
2346   rash

Les framboises sont des baies.
2347   raspberry

le rat
2348   rat

le hochet de bébé
2349   rattle

le serpent à sonnettes
2350   rattlesnake

Le corbeau a le plumage noir.
2351   raven

Elle semble **affamée**!
2352   ravenous

le ravin
2353   ravine

un œuf **cru**
2354   a raw egg

le rayon de soleil
2355   ray of sunlight

Le rasoir est très coupant.
2356   razor

atteindre
2357   to reach

lire
2358   to read

À vos marques... **prêts**... partez!
2359   ready

Est-ce que c'est un **vrai** diamant?
2360   real

comprendre, s'apercevoir, se rendre compte
2361   to realize/realise*

Es-tu **vraiment** là?
2362   Are you **really** here?

le derrière

2363   rear

le rétroviseur

2364   rearview mirror

raisonner

2365   to reason

raisonnable

C'est un prix **raisonnable**.
Julie, sois **raisonnable**
s'il te plaît.

*This is a reasonable price.
Julie, please be reasonable.*

2366   reasonable

se rebeller, se révolter

Les gens **se rebellent**
contre les impôts excessifs.
Spartacus **s'est révolté**
contre Rome.

*People do rebel against
taxes which are too high.
Spartacus rebelled against
Rome.*

2367   to rebel

Je ne **me souviens** pas.

2368   I do not recall.

Patricia vient de **recevoir**
un cadeau.

2369   to receive

récemment éclos

2370   recently hatched

la recette

2371   recipe

Elle **récite** un poème.

2372   to recite

un disque, un enregistrement

2373   record

le tourne-disque

2374   record player

guérir, récupérer

Julie a les oreillons mais
elle **guérira**.
J'ai **récupéré** tous les livres
qui étaient dehors.

*Julie has measles but she
will recover.
I recovered all the books
that were left outside.*

2375   to recover

le rectangle

2376   rectangle

rouge

2377   red

le roseau

2378   reed

le récif de corail

2379   reef

Comme ça **sent mauvais!**

2380   to reek

Le fil est enroulé sur **le
moulinet**.

2381   reel

un arbitre

2382   referee

le reflet

2383   reflection

Ne laisse pas **le réfrigérateur** ouvert!

2384   refrigerator

refuser

2385   to refuse

la région

2386   region

s'inscrire

2387   to register

regretter

2388   to regret

Les acteurs **répètent** une pièce.

2389   Actors **rehearse** a play.

le renne

2390   reindeer

les rênes du cheval

2391   reins

la parenté

2392   relatives

se reposer, se relaxer

2393   to relax

relâcher, libérer

2394   to release

Souviens-toi de te brosser les dents!

2395   Remember to brush your teeth.

une île **éloignée**

2396   remote island

Philippe **enlève** son chapeau.

2397   to remove

louer

Nous louons une maison.
Si tu n'as pas de voiture,
tu peux en **louer** une.

We rent a house.
If you do not have a car,
you can rent one.

2398   to rent

Blandine **répare** son vélo.

2399   to repair

Le perroquet **répète** tout.

2400   to repeat

Suzon **remplace** l'ampoule.

2401   to replace

Thierry pose une question
et Solange **répond**.

2402   to reply

le reptile

2403   reptile

secourir, sauver

2404   to rescue

le réservoir de pétrole

2405   reservoir

responsable

Julie, tu es **responsable** de ton petit frère.
Papa a vu le lait renversé et a demandé : «Qui est **responsable**?»

Julie, you are responsible for your little brother.
Dad saw the spilled milk and asked: "Who is responsible for this?"

2406   responsible

Paul **se repose** dans son fauteuil.

2407   to rest

le restaurant

2408   restaurant

rendre, revenir

Julie **rend** toujours ses livres de bibliothèque.
Jean est en voyage, mais il **reviendra** bientôt.

Julie always returns her library books.
John is travelling, but he will return soon.

2409   to return

Noémie fait **marche arrière**.

2410   reverse

le rhinocéros

2411   rhinoceros

la rhubarbe

2412   rhubarb

la rime

Voici un exemple de **rime** :
Une poule sur un mur
Qui picore du pain dur

2413   rhyme

la côte

2414   rib

Sais-tu faire un flot avec **un ruban**?

2415   ribbon

un bol de **riz**

2416   rice

riche

Les riches doivent aider les pauvres.
Les oranges sont **riches** en vitamines.

The rich must help the poor.
Oranges are rich in vitamins.

2417   rich

une énigme, la devinette

2418   riddle

monter à cheval

2419   to **ride** a horse

une arête, la crête

2420   ridge

ma main **droite**

2421   my **right** hand

droit, bien

Tourne à **droite** au coin.
Ce n'est pas **bien** de voler.

Turn right at the corner.
It is not right to steal.

2422   right

droitier 2423 right-handed	**la couenne** 2424 rind	**la bague** 2425 ring	L'oncle Pierre **sonne** à la porte. 2426 to ring
la patinoire 2427 rink	Papa **rince** la vaisselle. 2428 to rinse	**une émeute** 2429 riot	Il **a déchiré** son pantalon. 2430 to rip
La pomme est **mûre**. 2431 ripe	**l'ondulation, la ride** 2432 ripple	Le soleil **se lève**. 2433 The sun **rises**.	**le risque** Le météorologiste a dit qu'il y avait **un risque** de gelée. Sois prudent! Ne prends pas de **risques**! *The weatherman said there was a risk of frost.* *Be careful! Do not take any risks!* 2434 risk
des rivaux 2435 rivals	**La rivière** serpente. 2436 river	**La route** sinue. 2437 road	Le lion **rugit**. 2438 to roar
Le rôti sort du four. 2439 roast	**le voleur** 2440 robber	**le rouge-gorge** 2441 robin	**le rocher** 2442 rock

balancer, bercer	la fusée	le fauteuil à bascule	la canne à pêche
2443 to rock	2444 rocket	2445 rocking chair	2446 rod

le rouleau de papier	rouler	le patin à roulettes	le rouleau à pâtisserie
2447 roll	2448 to roll	2449 roller skate	2450 rolling pin

Le toit est fait de tuiles.	la chambre, la pièce	Le coq se perche pour la nuit.	la racine
2451 roof	2452 room	2453 to roost	2454 root

la corde	La rose a des épines.	le romarin	Mélanie a les joues roses.
2455 rope	2456 rose	2457 rosemary	2458 rosy

La pomme est pourrie.	râpeux, rugueux	Le bouton est rond.	une rangée de 4 boutons
2459 rotten apple	2460 rough	2461 round	2462 4 buttons in a row

Elle **rame** plus vite que Luc.

2463　to row

un habit **royal**

2464　royal

Le pneu et la balle sont en **caoutchouc**.

2465　rubber

les déchets, les détritus

2466　rubbish

Le rubis est une pierre rouge.

2467　ruby

le gouvernail

2468　rudder

Il est **malpoli**.

2469　He is rude.

le terrain **accidenté**

2470　rugged terrain

les ruines d'un ancien château

2471　ruin

la règle, le règne

Maman et Papa décident **des règles** de conduite à la maison. Certains pays sont sous **le règne** d'un roi.

Mother and Father make the rules in this house.
Some countries are under the rule of a king.

2472　rule

Le souverain règne.

2473　ruler

J'entends **un grondement**.

2474　I hear a rumble.

courir

2475　to run

se sauver

2476　to run away

écraser

2477　to run over

s'épuiser, arriver au bout de ses forces

2478　to run out of energy

Elle se **précipite** pour attraper l'autobus.

2479　to rush

Le robot est couvert de **rouille**.

2480　rust

une ornière

2481　rut

Le seigle pousse dans les champs.

2482　rye

le sac de farine

2483   sack

La vérité est un principe **sacré**.

2484   Truth is a **sacred** principle.

triste

2485   sad

la selle

2486   saddle

Qu'est-ce qu'il y a dans **le coffre-fort**?

2487   safe

Le vent gonfle **la voile**.

2488   sail

la planche à voile

2489   sailboard

Le voilier vogue sur l'eau.

2490   sailboat/sailing boat*

le marin

2491   sailor

la salade

2492   salad

les soldes

2493   sale

le saumon

2494   salmon

le sel et le poivre

2495   salt

saluer

2496   to salute

pareil, **identique**

2497   same

le sable

2498   sand

la sandale

2499   sandal

Julie s'est préparé **un sandwich**.

2500   sandwich

la sève de l'érable

2501   sap

la sardine

2502   sardine

Le satellite tourne autour de la terre.

2503   satellite

une robe de satin

2504   satin dress

samedi

Le samedi, Julie ne va pas à l'école et peut jouer.

Julie can play on Saturday because she does not go to school.

2505   Saturday

la sauce

2506   sauce/gravy*

la saucisse

2507   sausage

J'économise mon argent.

2508   I save my money.

La scie a des dents.

2509   saw

la sciure

2511   sawdust

Je dis ce que je pense.

2512   I say what I think.

L'artiste est allongé sur son échafaudage.

2513   scaffolding

scier du bois

2510   to saw

échauder, ébouillanter

2514   to scald

La balance a deux plateaux.

2515   scale

la pétoncle, la coquille Saint-Jacques

2516   scallop

le cuir chevelu

2517   scalp

l'homme à la cicatrice

2518   scar

Elle trouve un malin plaisir à l'effrayer.

2519   to scare

Un épouvantail sert à effrayer les oiseaux.

2520   scarecrow

une écharpe bien chaude

2521   scarf

écarlate

2522   scarlet

la scène d'un crime

2523   scene of a crime

le paysage

2524   scenery

l'érudition, la bourse d'études

2525   scholarship

une école de village

2526   school

la goélette

2527   schooner

les ciseaux

2528   scissors

écoper, ramasser

2529   to scoop

le scooter

2530   scooter

Le papier est **roussi** par la flamme.

2531   scorched paper

marquer un but

2532   to score

le scout

2533   scout

des bouts de papier

2534   scraps of paper

une **éraflure**, une **égratignure**

2535   scrape

le grattoir, la gratte

2536   scraper

la griffure

2537   scratch

la moustiquaire

2538   screen

la vis

2539   screw

le tournevis

2540   screwdriver

frotter, récurer

2541   to scrub

Le sculpteur taille la pierre.

2542　　sculptor

un hippocampe

2543　　seahorse

la mer Adriatique

2544　　Adriatic sea

la mouette, le goéland

2545　　seagull

le phoque

2546　　seal

la couture

2547　　seam

Que **cherche**-t-il dans l'herbe?

2548　　to search

le projecteur

2549　　searchlight

les saisons

Les quatre **saisons** de l'année sont le printemps, l'été, l'automne et l'hiver.

The four seasons are spring, summer, autumn and winter.

2550　　seasons

le siège

2551　　seat

Julie a mis sa **ceinture** de sécurité.

2552　　seatbelt

une algue

2553　　seaweed

le second

2554　　second

J'ai **un secret**.

2555　　I have a secret.

voir

2556　　to see

la bascule, la balance

2557　　see-saw

De **la graine** naît la plante.

2558　　seed

Il **semble** mort mais il ne l'est peut-être pas.

2559　　It seems to be dead.

saisir

2560　　to seize

Tu es **égoïste**, Marcel!

2561　　You are selfish.

Marie **vend** des fruits.

2562   to sell

le demi-cercle

2563   semicircle

envoyer, expédier

2564   to send

une peau **sensible**

2565   sensitive skin

la phrase, la peine

Est-ce que tu sais faire
une phrase?
Le voleur a été condamné
à **une peine** de prison.

Can you make a sentence?
The robber received a
prison sentence.

2566   sentence

la sentinelle

2567   sentry

Septembre est le neuvième
mois de l'année.

2568   September

servir un repas

2569   to serve

sept

2570   seven

le septième

2571   seventh

plusieurs

2572   several

Elle **coud** avec du fil
et une aiguille.

2573   to sew

la machine à coudre

2574   sewing machine

usé, élimé

2575   shabby

la cabane

2576   shack

une ombre

2577   shadow

un chien à **longs poils**

2578   shaggy

secouer

2579   to shake

une eau **peu profonde**

2580   shallow water

Maman se lave les cheveux
avec du **shampooing**.

2581   shampoo

Nous pouvons **partager**.

2582   to share

Crois-tu que **le requin** apprend à voler?

2583   shark

tranchant, aiguisé

2584   sharp

Un affiloir sert à aiguiser.

2585   knife sharpener

fracasser, briser en éclats

2588   to shatter

se raser

2589   to shave

les cisailles

2590   shears

une affûteuse à patins

2586   skate sharpener

le fourreau

2591   sheath

Julie compte **des moutons** pour s'endormir

2592   sheep

le drap du lit

2593   sheet

le taille-crayons

2587   pencil sharpener

une étagère

2594   shelf

la coquille, le coquillage

2595   shell

L'insecte a trouvé **un abri**.

2596   shelter

Le berger, garde les moutons.

2597   shepherd

Le bouclier protège le guerrier.

2598   shield

le devant de la jambe

2599   shin

Le soleil **brille** de tous ses rayons.

2600   to shine

le bardeau

2601   shingle

Le zona est une maladie.

2602   shingles

Les diamants de la couronne sont **brillants**.

2603   shiny

le bateau, le navire

2604   ship

Robinson a fait **naufrage**.

2605   shipwreck

la chemise

2606   shirt

frissonner, grelotter

2607   to shiver

le choc

2608   shock

les chaussures, les souliers

2609   shoes

Est-ce que tu sais nouer tes **lacets**?

2610   shoelace

le cordonnier

2611   shoemaker

tirer

2612   to shoot

le magasin, la boutique

2613   shop

le marchand, le commerçant

2614   shopkeeper

la vitrine

2615   shop window

le rivage

2616   shore

petit, court

2617   short

un short

2618   shorts

une épaule

2619   shoulder

crier

2620   to shout

Il ne faut pas **pousser** les gens.

2621   to shove

la pelle pour enlever la neige

2622   shovel

montrer

2623   to show

parader, se pavaner

2624   to show off

Il a fini par **se montrer**.

2625   to show up/appear*

Julien prend **une douche**.

2626   shower

pousser des cris aigus

2627   to shriek

la crevette

2628   shrimp

Comme sa chemise **a rétréci!**

2629   to shrink

un arbuste

2630   shrub

battre, mélanger les cartes

2631   shuffle

La nuit, on ferme **les volets**.

2632   shutters

timide

2633   shy

malade

2634   sick

le côté sans fenêtres

2635   side

Julie marche toujours sur **le trottoir**.

2636   sidewalk/pavement*

soupirer de fatigue, de tristesse

2637   to sigh

la pancarte

2638   sign

signaler

2639   to signal

la signature

2640   signature

silencieux

Julie n'est pas souvent **silencieuse**.
Une nuit **silencieuse** est une nuit tranquille.

*Julie is not silent very often.
A silent night is
a quiet night.*

2641   silent

le rebord de la fenêtre

2642   sill

---

idiot, stupide

Sébastien pense que Julie est complètement **idiote**. Julie pense que Sébastien fait des choses **stupides**.

Sébastien thinks Julie is silly.
Julie thinks Sébastien does silly things.

2643   silly

L'argent est un métal précieux.

2644   silver

---

simple

C'est la vérité pure et **simple**.
Il y a une solution très **simple**.

That is the truth, pure and simple.
There is a very simple solution.

2645   simple

---

chanter

2646   to sing

---

singulier

«Un» est **singulier**.
«Plusieurs» est pluriel.

"One" is singular.
"Several" is plural.

2647   singular

---

un évier de cuisine

2648   sink

Au secours! Le bateau coule.

2649   to sink

---

siroter, boire à petites gorgées

2650   to sip

---

la sirène

2651   siren

Paule est la sœur de Laurent.

2652   sister

être assis

2653   to sit

---

six

2654   six

---

le sixième

2655   sixth

Est-ce que c'est ma taille?

2656   size

---

patiner

2657   to skate

---

la planche à roulettes

2658   skateboard

Un squelette dans le placard?!

2659   skeleton

L'artiste dessine.

2660   to sketch

---

les skis

2661   skis

skier	Horace a presque **dérapé**.	**la peau**	**sauter** à la corde
2662 to ski	2663 to skid	2664 skin	2665 to skip
Le capitaine tient le gouvernail.	**la jupe**	**le crâne**	**Le ciel** est nuageux.
2666 skipper/captain*	2667 skirt	2668 skull	2669 sky
une alouette	**le gratte-ciel**	Barnabé **a claqué** la porte.	un plancher **incliné**
2670 skylark	2671 skyscraper	2672 to slam	2673 slanting floor
donner une claque, gifler	**taillader, sabrer**	**une ardoise**	**La luge** dévale la pente.
2674 to slap	2675 to slash	2676 slate	2677 sled/sleigh*
Zorro **dort** avec son sabre.	**le sac de couchage, le duvet**	Paul se sent tout **somnolent**.	**la neige fondante**
2678 to sleep	2679 sleeping bag	2680 sleepy	2681 sleet

la manche

2682   sleeve

le toboggan

2683   slide

L'une est **mince**,
l'autre est **grosse**.

2684   slim

Le ver a un corps **visqueux**.

2685   slimy

Il a le bras en **écharpe**.

2686   sling

la **fronde**, le **lance-pierre**

2687   slingshot/catapult*

glisser

2688   to slip

la pantoufle

2689   slipper

glissant

2690   slippery

Comme il est **malpropre**!

2691   slob

La pente de la montagne
est rude.

2692   slope

la fente

2693   slot

Il ne faut pas
se tenir voûté.

2694   to slouch

ralentir

Ralentis Papa! Tu roules
trop vite!
La voiture **ralentit** au coin
de la rue.

*Slow down, Dad! You are
going too fast.
The car slows down at
the corner.*

2695   to slow down

la neige à demi-fondue

2696   slush

L'un est **petit**,
l'autre est **grand**.

2697   small

intelligent, **élégant**

Julie a fait quelque chose
de très **intelligent**.
Elle porte une robe très
élégante.

*Julie did a very smart thing.
because she passed
her exam.
She is wearing a very smart
dress.*

2698   smart/clever*

écraser, **démolir**

2699   to smash

barbouiller, **salir**

2700   to smear

Comme cette fleur **sent** bon!

2701   to smell

La mouffette a une odeur **nauséabonde**!

2702   smelly

fumer

2703   to smoke

lisse, en douceur

La glace sur laquelle Julie patine est bien **lisse**.
Un bon pilote sait atterrir **en douceur**.

The ice Julie is skating on is very smooth.
A good pilot makes smooth landings.

2704   smooth

Noémie aime **goûter** entre les repas.

2705   to have a snack

un escargot

2706   snail

le serpent

2707   snake

se casser avec un bruit sec

2708   to snap

les espadrilles de sport

2709   sneakers/trainers*

La poussière l'a fait **éternuer**.

2710   to sneeze

le masque et **le tube**

2711   snorkel

La neige tombe du ciel.

2712   snow

le flocon de neige

2713   snowflake

les raquettes

2714   snowshoes

Lave-toi les mains avec du **savon**!

2715   soap

le foot-ball

2716   soccer

la chaussette

2717   sock

la prise de courant

2718   socket

le sofa, le canapé

2719   sofa/couch*

Sacha a la fourrure **douce**.

2720   soft

le soldat

2721   soldier

la sole

2722   sole

Elle résout un problème.

2723   She **solves** the problem.

faire la culbute

2724   to **somersault**

le père et le fils

2725   son

le chant, la chanson

2726   song

bientôt

Il fera **bientôt** nuit.
Julie sera **bientôt** de retour
à la maison.

Soon it will be dark.
Julie will be home soon.

2727   soon

Le sorcier jette un
mauvais sort.

2728   sorcerer

Mon bras est douloureux.

2729   My arm is **sore**.

L'oseille a un goût acide.

2730   sorrel

Milou est absolument **navré**.

2731   sorry

Il **trie** les bons des mauvais.

2732   to **sort**

la soupe

2733   soup

Le citron est **acide**.

2734   sour

le sud

2735   south

La truie est la mère
des porcelets.

2736   sow

semer

2737   to **sow**

le vaisseau spatial

2738   spaceship

La bêche sert à jardiner.

2739   spade

donner la fessée

2740   to **spank**

la roue de secours

2741   spare tire/tyre*

une étincelle	Ses bagues **étincellent** au soleil.	**le moineau**	Quelle langue **parlent**-ils?
2742 spark	2743 to sparkle	2744 sparrow	2745 to speak
la lance	La tortue a du mal à **accélérer**.	Alice va **épeler** son prénom.	**dépenser** de l'argent
2746 spear	2747 to speed up	2748 to spell	2749 to spend
la sphère	**épicé**	Une **araignée** tisse sa toile.	**le piquant**
2750 sphere	2751 spicy	2752 spider	2753 spike
renverser, répandre	La toupie **tourne**.	**les épinards**	**la colonne vertébrale**
2754 to spill	2755 to spin	2756 spinach	2757 spine
la spirale	**la flèche** de l'église	Ce n'est pas poli de **cracher**!	**éclabousser**
2758 spiral	2759 spire	2760 to spit	2761 to splash

un éclat de bois

2762   splinter

Les fruits sont **gâtés**.

2763   spoiled/rotten* fruit

une éponge

2764   sponge

la bobine de fil

2765   spool/reel*

la cuillère

2766   spoon

D'où vient cette vilaine **tache?**

2767   spot

le bec de la théière

2768   spout

se faire une entorse

2769   to sprain

vaporiser

2770   to spray

étaler

2771   to spread

le ressort

2772   spring

Le printemps est enfin arrivé!

2773   spring

saupoudrer

2775   to sprinkle

sprinter, faire une course de vitesse

2776   to sprint

le sapin, une épinette

2777   spruce

La source coule vite.

2774   spring

le carré

2778   square

la courge, la gourde

2779   squash

s'accroupir

2780   to squat

Julie **serre** son ami dans ses bras.

2781   to squeeze

le calmar
2782   squid

un écureuil
2783   squirrel

faire gicler
2784   to squirt

une écurie à chevaux
2785   stable

la scène du théâtre
2786   stage

la tache
2787   stain

Où mène l'escalier?
2788   staircase

un piquet en bois
2789   wooden stake

rassis
Je n'aime pas le pain rassis, je préfère le pain frais.

I do not like stale bread, I prefer fresh bread.

2790   stale bread

la branche de céleri
2791   celery stalk

Un étalon est un cheval mâle.
2792   stallion

le timbre
2793   stamp

être debout, se tenir debout
2794   to stand

une étoile
2795   star

Julie regarde fixement devant elle.
2796   to stare

un étourneau
2797   starling

faire démarrer une voiture
2798   to start a car

mourir de faim
Quand Julie rentre de l'école, elle crie: «Je meurs de faim!» Elle est affamée, mais elle ne va pas vraiment mourir de faim.

When Julie comes back from school, she always shouts: "I'm starving." She is very hungry, but she will not really starve.

2799   to starve

la station-service
2800   gas/petrol* station

la gare
2801   train/railway* station

la statue

2802   statue

Médor! **Reste** là!

2803   **S**tay there!

un steak, un bifteck

2804   steak

Le cambrioleur **vole**.

2805   to **s**teal

la vapeur

2806   steam

Les couteaux sont en **acier**.

2807   **K**inves are made of **s**teel.

escarpé, à pic

2808   steep

le bœuf

2809   steer/bullock*

la tige de la rose

2811   stem

la marche

2812   step

Elle **a marché dans** la flaque.

2813   to step in

conduire, diriger

2810   to steer

Papa a préparé **un ragoût**.

2815   stew

la baguette

2816   stick

sortir une minute

2814   to step out

Didier a les mains **collantes**.

2817   sticky

raide, dur

Oncle Jean a la jambe **raide**.
Cette brosse à dents est trop **dure**.

Uncle Jean has a stiff leg.
This toothbrush is too stiff.

2818   stiff

Une abeille l'**a piquée**.

2819   to **s**ting

la piqûre

2820   sting

sentir très mauvais

2821   to **s**tink

Remue avant de goûter!

2822   to stir

les bas

2823   stockings

charger une chaudière

2824   to stoke

un estomac

2825   stomach

le caillou, ia pierre

2826   stone

L'araignée descend vers **le tabouret**.

2827   stool

Elle **se baisse** pour ramasser la balle.

2828   to stoop/bend down*

un arrêt, le stop

2829   stop

le magasin

CRAWZI

2832   store/shop*

la cigogne

2833   stork

un orage, la tempête

2834   storm

Il **arrête** le train.

2830   He **stops** the train.

Tante Annie lit **une histoire**.

2835   story

la cuisinière

2836   stove/cooker*

droit, rectiligne

2837   straight

L'avion a fait **une escale**.

2831   to stop over

filtrer

2838   to strain

forcer, peiner

2839   to strain

Quel **étrange** animal!

2840   strange

Jo s'est trop approché. Le singe va l'**étrangler**.

2841   to strangle

la bretelle

2842   strap

Est-ce que tu aimes boire avec **une paille**?

2843   straw

la fraise

2844   strawberry

le cours d'eau, la rivière

2845   stream

la banderole, le fanion

2846   streamer/pennant*

La rue est déserte.

2847   street

le réverbère

2848   street light/lamp*

étirer

2849   to stretch

le brancard, la civière

2850   stretcher

la grève

Les ouvriers sont en **grève** parce qu'ils veulent une augmentation.

The workers are on strike for more money.

2851   strike

Il ne faut pas **frapper** les gens.

2852   to strike

La ficelle est enroulée sur la bobine.

2853   string

une serviette à **rayures**

2854   stripe

Il est très **fort**.

2855   strong

un étudiant

2856   student

Il **étudie** sagement.

2857   to study

un animal **rembourré**

2858   a stuffed animal

la souche

2859   stump

Le sous-marin navigue sous l'eau.

2860   submarine

soustraire

2861   to subtract

sucer
2862   to suck

soudain, brusquement
Il a **soudain** commencé
à pleuvoir.
Amélie est **brusquement**
partie.

Suddenly, it began to rain.
Amélie left suddenly.

2863   suddenly

Ne mange pas trop de **sucre**!
2864   sugar

Louis porte **un costume**.
2865   suit

la valise
2866   suitcase

un été au bord de la mer
2867   summer

le soleil
2868   sun

dimanche
Dimanche est l'un des
jours de la semaine.
Tous les **dimanches**,
Maman fait un gâteau.

Sunday is one of the days
of the week.
Every Sunday, Mother
bakes a cake.

2869   Sunday

Le cadran solaire
indique l'heure.
2870   sundial

Le tournesol fait face au soleil.
2871   sunflower

le lever du soleil
2872   sunrise

le coucher du soleil
2873   sunset

Aude fait les courses
au **supermarché**.
2874   supermarket

le dîner, le souper
2875   supper/dinner*

sûr, certain
Je suis **sûr** qu'il fera
beau demain.
C'est un moyen **certain**
de gagner.

I am sure it will be
nice tomorrow.
That is a sure way to win.

2876   sure

la surface
2877   surface

le chirurgien
2878   surgeon

le nom de famille
Mon prénom est Julie, mon
nom de famille est Dubois.

My first name is Julie and
my surname is Dubois.

2879   surname

la surprise-partie
2880   surprise party

Ne tirez pas! Je **me rends**.
2881   to surrender

entourer, encercler

2882   to surround

Les bretelles retiennent son pantalon.

2883   suspenders/braces*

avaler

2884   to swallow

Le cygne est majestueux.

2885   swan

échanger, troquer

2886   to swap

un essaim d'abeilles en colère

2887   swarm

Il **transpire** à grosses gouttes.

2888   to sweat

le chandail, le tricot

2889   sweater/sweatshirt*

balayer

2890   to sweep

sucré

2891   sweet

Heureusement, l'auto **a fait un écart**.

2892   to swerve

André sait bien **nager**.

2893   to swim

la balançoire

2894   swing

se balancer

2895   to swing

un interrupteur

2896   switch

allumer, éteindre

Allume la lumière, s'il te plaît.
Il vaut mieux **éteindre** la télévision.

Switch on the light, please. It is best to switch off the television.

2897   to switch

s'abattre, fondre sur une proie

2898   to swoop

une épée

2899   sword

le sycomore

2900   sycamore

Le sirop d'érable est bon avec des gaufres!

2901   syrup

T

La tasse est sur **la table**.

2902   table

La nappe a des carreaux bleus et blancs.

2903   tablecloth

le comprimé

2904   tablet

la pointe, la punaise

2905   tack

s'attaquer à, plaquer

Julie doit **s'attaquer à** ce problème au plus vite.
Alain **a plaqué** Yves au sol durant la partie de rugby.

Julie must tackle that problem as soon as possible.
Alain tackled Yves during the rugby match.

2906   to tackle

Le têtard deviendra grenouille.

2907   tadpole

Il a **la queue** touffue.

2908   tail

prendre

2910   to take

démonter

2911   to take apart

emporter

2912   to take away

rapporter

2913   to take back

enlever

2914   to take off

décoller

2915   to take off

sortir

2916   to take out

le repas à emporter

2917   take-out/take-away*

Le tailleur fait des vêtements.

2909   tailor

le récit, une histoire

2918   tale

le talent

Sylvie a beaucoup de **talent** pour la danse.
Pour bien danser, il faut du **talent** et de l'effort.

Sylvie has a great talent for dancing.
Dance requires both talent and hard work.

2919   talent

parler

2920   to talk

grand, haut

2921   tall

le tambourin

2922   tambourine

dompté, apprivoisé

2923   tame

Elle a **un** beau **bronzage.**

2924   tan

la mandarine

2925   tangerine

Le fil est tout **emmêlé!**

2926   tangled

le réservoir, la citerne

2927   tank

**le pétrolier,
le navire-citerne**

2928   tanker

Le robinet fuit goutte à goutte.

2929   tap

le ruban adhésif

2930   tape

fixer avec du ruban adhésif

2931   to tape

le magnétophone et la
cassette

2932   tape recorder

le goudron

2933   tar

en plein dans **la cible**

2934   target

l'estragon

2935   tarragon

la tarte, la tartelette

2936   tart

la tâche, le travail

2937   task

Goûte et dis-moi si c'est bon!

2938   to taste

succulent, savoureux

C'était un repas **succulent.**
La tarte était
savoureuse.

*This was a tasty meal.
The tart was very tasty.*

2939   tasty

le taxi

2940   taxi

une tasse de **thé**	Mademoiselle Blanche **enseigne** le calcul.	C'est notre **institutrice**.	**une équipe** inséparable
2941 a cup of **tea**	2942 to **teach**	2943 **teacher**	2944 **team**
la théière	**la larme**	**déchirer**	Il ne faut jamais **arracher** les pages!
2945 **teapot**	2946 **tear**	2947 to **tear**	2948 to **tear** out
le télégramme	**le téléphone**	Margot aime **téléphoner** à ses amis.	**Le téléscope** est braqué vers le ciel.
2949 **telegram**	2950 **telephone**	2951 to **telephone**	2952 **telescope**
La télévision, c'est la télé ou la TV.	Elle lui **dit** ce qu'elle pense.	**le caractère** Christophe a mauvais **caractère**. Il n'arrive pas à rester calme. *Christophe has a bad temper.* *He cannot control his temper.*	Le thermomètre marque **la température**.
2953 **television**	2954 to **tell**	2955 **temper**	2956 **temperature**
dix pommes	la raquette et la balle de **tennis**	la chaussure de **tennis**	Julie a dormi sous **la tente.**
2957 **ten** apples	2958 **tennis** racquet and ball	2959 **tennis** shoe	2960 **tent**

le dixième escargot

2961   tenth

le terminal de l'ordinateur

2962   terminal

essayer l'eau

2963   to **test** the water

Elle le **remercie** de tout cœur.

2964   to thank

dégeler

2965   to thaw

le théâtre

2966   theater/theatre*

La balle est **là**!

2967   there

Le thermomètre est gradué.

2968   thermometer

Cet arbre a un tronc **épais**.

2969   thick

Le voleur porte un masque.

2970   thief

la cuisse

2971   thigh

le dé à coudre

2972   thimble

Le tronc de cet arbre est **mince**.

2973   thin

la chose

Une personne, ce n'est pas **une chose**.
Julie dit beaucoup de **choses** amusantes.

A person is not a thing. Julie says many funny things.

2974   thing

penser

2975   to **think**

le troisième escargot

2976   third

Il **a soif**, il est **assoiffé**.

2977   thirsty

Attention! **Le chardon** est piquant.

2978   thistle

une épine

2979   thorn

le fil

2980   thread

Est-ce que tu sais **enfiler** une aiguille?	**trois** pommes	**le seuil** de la porte	**la gorge**
2981 to thread	2982 three	2983 threshold	2984 throat
le trône de la reine	**jeter**	Il a le mal de mer et il **vomit**.	**le pouce**
2985 throne	2986 to throw	2987 to throw up/be sick*	2988 thumb
un coup de **tonnerre** assourdissant	**un orage**	**jeudi** **Jeudi** est le jour de la semaine qui vient après mercredi. Julie va à sa leçon de natation **le jeudi**. *Thursday is the day after Wednesday.* *Julie goes to swimming class on Thursday.*	Maman épice le rôti avec du **thym**.
2989 thunder	2990 thunderstorm	2991 Thursday	2992 thyme
le billet de métro	**chatouiller**	**propre, soigneux**	Papa a noué sa **cravate**.
2993 ticket	2994 to tickle	2995 tidy	2996 tie
Le tigre va à la chasse.	Comme elle **serre** sa ceinture!	**le carrelage**	**attacher, nouer**
2998 tiger	2999 to tighten	3000 tiles	2997 to tie

Le bateau **penche** dangereusement.

3001   to tilt

Quelle **heure** est-il?

3002   What **time** is it?

minuscule

3003   tiny

Le bateau **a chaviré**.

3004   to tip

marcher sur la pointe des pieds

3006   tiptoe

Est-ce que **le pneu** est assez gonflé?

3007   tire/tyre*

fatigué, las

3008   tired

donner un pourboire

3005   to tip

Le crapaud vit près de la mare.

3009   toad

le toast, le pain grillé

3010   toast

le grille-pain

3011   toaster

aujourd'hui

L'école commence **aujourd'hui**.
Aujourd'hui, Julie se lève tôt pour préparer son petit déjeuner.

School starts today.
Today Julie gets up early to make her breakfast.

3012   today

les orteils

3013   toes

Nous sommes assis **ensemble**.

3014   We are sitting **together**.

les toilettes

3015   toilet

la tomate

3016   tomato

la tombe

3017   tomb

demain

Demain suit aujourd'hui.
Demain, Julie va voir les dinosaures au musée.

Today is followed by tomorrow.
Tomorrow, Julie is going to see the dinosaurs at the museum.

3018   tomorrow

les pinces

3019   tongs

Voyons! Ne tire pas **la langue**!

3020   tongue

Il pèse une tonne.	**les amygdales**	**les outils** du bricoleur	Elle a de belles **dents**.
3021 It weighs a **ton**.	3022 tonsils	3023 tools	3024 tooth
le mal de dents	**la brosse à dents**	**le dentifrice**	**le sommet, le haut**
3025 toothache	3026 toothbrush	3027 toothpaste	3028 top
tomber, dégringoler	**le flambeau** olympique	**La tornade** balaie tout sur son passage.	**La toupie** tourne sur elle-même.
3030 to topple	3031 torch	3032 tornado	3029 top
le torrent	**La tortue** a une carapace.	**lancer, jeter**	**toucher**
3033 torrent	3034 tortoise	3035 to toss	3036 to touch
Je suis dur.	Le camion **remorque** l'auto.	Julie s'essuie avec **la serviette**.	**la tour** la plus haute au monde
3037 I am **tough**.	3038 to tow	3039 towel	3040 tower

la ville
3041   town

Ramasse tes **jouets** s'il te plaît!
3042   toys

tracer
3043   to trace

Le train suit **la voie** ferrée.
3044   track

le tracteur
3045   tractor

échanger, faire des affaires
3046   to trade

La circulation est dense.
3047   traffic

les feux de circulation
3048   traffic light

Il est sur **la bonne piste**.
3049   trail

Qu'est-ce qu'il y a dans **la remorque**?
3050   trailer

le train
3051   train

Elle **dresse** son chien.
3052   to train

le vagabond
3053   tramp

Il ne faut pas **piétiner** les fleurs!
3054   to trample

le tremplin
3055   trampoline

Le verre que tient la maman de Julie est **transparent**.
3056   transparent

transporter
3057   to transport

le camion-plateau, le fardier
3058   transporter/lorry*

La souris se méfie du **piège**.
3059   trap

le trapèze
3060   trapeze

Tante Annie **voyage** en train.

3061   to travel

Ne renverse pas **le plateau**!

3062   tray

la bande de roulement du pneu

3063   tread

le trésor

3064   treasure

un arbre

3065   tree

Judith **tremble** de peur.

3066   to tremble

la tranchée

3067   trench

le procès

3068   trial

Le triangle a trois côtés.

3069   triangle

le tour, le truc

3070   trick

couler goutte à goutte

3071   to trickle

Le tricycle a trois roues.

3072   tricycle

la détente, la gachette du pistolet

3073   trigger

Le coiffeur lui **égalise** les cheveux.

3074   to trim

un voyage court

3075   a short trip

trébucher

3076   to trip

le trolleybus

3077   trolley bus

Le poulain aime **trotter** et galoper.

3078   to trot

une auge à cochons

3079   trough

le pantalon

3080   trousers

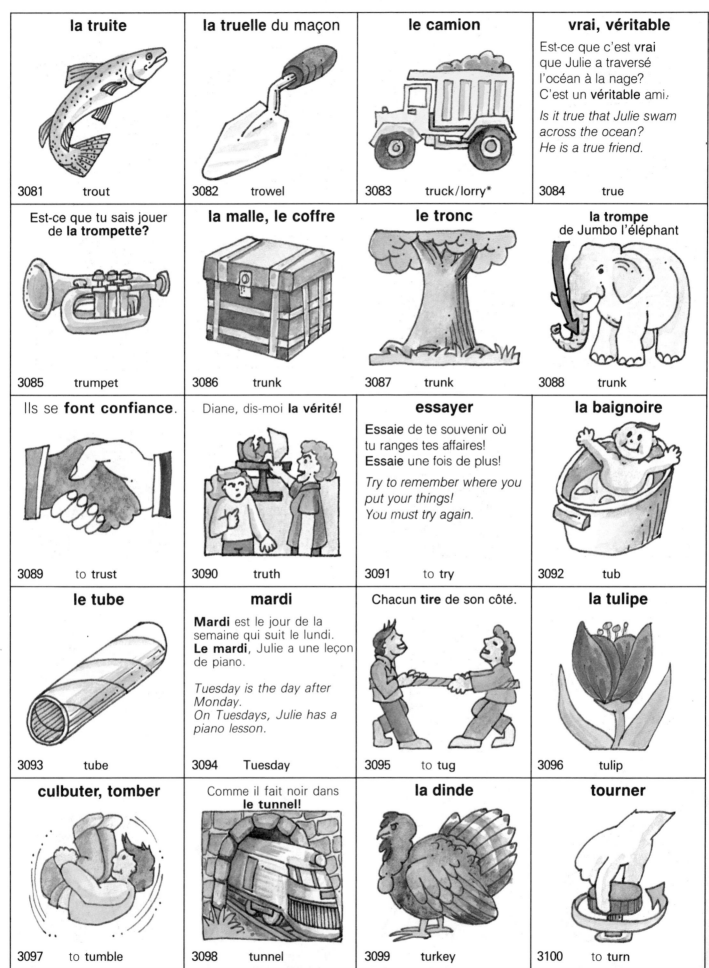

la truite
3081   trout

la truelle du maçon
3082   trowel

le camion
3083   truck/lorry*

vrai, véritable
Est-ce que c'est **vrai** que Julie a traversé l'océan à la nage? C'est un **véritable** ami.

Is it true that Julie swam across the ocean? He is a true friend.

3084   true

Est-ce que tu sais jouer de **la trompette**?

3085   trumpet

la malle, le coffre
3086   trunk

le tronc
3087   trunk

la trompe
de Jumbo l'éléphant

3088   trunk

Ils se **font confiance**.

3089   to trust

Diane, dis-moi **la vérité!**

3090   truth

essayer
Essaie de te souvenir où tu ranges tes affaires! **Essaie** une fois de plus!

Try to remember where you put your things! You must try again.

3091   to try

la baignoire
3092   tub

le tube
3093   tube

mardi
Mardi est le jour de la semaine qui suit le lundi. **Le mardi**, Julie a une leçon de piano.

Tuesday is the day after Monday. On Tuesdays, Julie has a piano lesson.

3094   Tuesday

Chacun **tire** de son côté.

3095   to tug

la tulipe
3096   tulip

culbuter, tomber
3097   to tumble

Comme il fait noir dans **le tunnel!**

3098   tunnel

la dinde
3099   turkey

tourner
3100   to turn

éteindre

3101   to **turn off**

allumer

3102   to **turn on**

devenir, tourner

Quelle jolie petite fille elle **est devenue**.
Les choses **ont** bien **tourné**.

What a pretty girl she turned out to be!
Things turned out well.

3103   to **turn out**

tourner, retourner

3104   to **turn over**

le navet

3105   turnip

le tourne-disque

3106   turntable

turquoise

3107   turquoise

Le guetteur est dans **la tourelle**.

3108   turret

la tortue

3109   turtle

Les défenses de l'éléphant sont en ivoire.

3110   tusk

la pince à épiler

3111   tweezers

deux fois

Julie est allée au zoo **deux fois**.
Caroline a **deux fois** plus de livres que moi.

Julie has been to the zoo twice.
Caroline has twice as many books as I.

3112   twice

la brindille

3113   twig

Les jumeaux sont identiques.

3114   twins

Les étoiles **scintillent**.

3115   Stars twinkle.

tourner, tournoyer

3116   to twirl

tordre, tortiller

3117   to twist

deux

3118   two

écrire à la machine, dactylographier

3119   to type

la machine à écrire

3120   typewriter

Elle est **laide** mais si gentille.

3121   ugly

le parapluie

3122   umbrella

un oncle

Mon **oncle** est le frère de ma mère.
Mon autre **oncle** est le frère de mon père.

My uncle is my mother's brother.
My other uncle is my father's brother.

3123   uncle

sous, moins de

Julie se cache **sous** les couvertures.
Les enfants de **moins de** 5 ans ne peuvent pas y aller.

Julie is hiding under the covers.
Children under 5 cannot go.

3124   under

comprendre

3125   to understand

les sous-vêtements

3126   underwear

se déshabiller

3127   to undress

triste, malheureux

3128   unhappy

La licorne n'existe que dans les fables.

3129   unicorn

L'oncle Richard porte **un uniforme**.

3130   uniform

Fabienne est diplômée de **l'université**.

3131   university

Qu'est-ce que le camion **décharge**?

3132   to unload

déverrouiller

3133   to unlock

déballer

3134   to unwrap

debout

3135   upright

à l'envers

3136   upside-down

Maman **utilise** du poivre pour faire la cuisine.

3137   to use

Elle **a tout utilisé** le poivre.

3138   to use up

Ce couteau de poche est très **utile**.

3139   useful

Vivent les vacances!

3140 vacation/holiday*

la vapeur

3141 vapor/vapour*

Anatole **vernit** le bois pour le protéger.

3142 to varnish

Julie a fait cadeau d'**un vase** à sa maman.

3143 vase

une côtelette de **veau**

3144 veal

les légumes

3145 vegetable

le véhicule

3146 vehicle

le voile, la voilette

3147 veil

la veine

3148 vein

le venin

Le **venin** est le poison des serpents vénimeux. Certains insectes ont aussi du **venin**.

Venom is the poison of poisonous snakes. Some insects also have venom.

3149 venom

Une ligne droite, de haut en bas, est **verticale**.

3150 vertical

très

Julie pense que son petit frère est **très** malin. La soupe sera prête **très** bientôt.

Julie thinks her little brother is very clever. Very soon the soup will be ready.

3151 very

le gilet

3152 vest/waistcoat*

Le vétérinaire soigne les animaux.

3153 veterinarian/veterinary surgeon*

la victime du crime

3154 victim

le magnétoscope

3155 video recorder

Il ne faut pas jouer avec **une bande vidéo**.

3156 video tape

la vue

Quelle belle **vue** nous avons du sommet de la montagne! Chacun de nous a son point de **vue**.

What a wonderful view from the top of the mountain! We each have our own point of view.

3157 view

le village

3158 village

le bandit, le gredin

3159   villain

Les raisins sont les fruits de **la vigne**.

3160   vine

Du **vinaigre** sur les frites!

3161   vinegar

Grand-mère aime le parfum de **la violette**.

3162   violet

le violon

3163   violin

Il faut **un visa** pour aller à l'étranger.

3164   visa

visible

Il y a beaucoup de nuages ce soir et les étoiles sont à peine **visibles**.
On ne peut pas voir du tout un homme **invisible**.

There are many clouds tonight and the stars are barely visible.
An invisible man cannot be seen.

3165   visible

visiter, rendre visite

3166   to visit

la visière

3167   visor

le vocabulaire

Julie a **un vocabulaire** riche; elle sait beaucoup de mots.
Ce dictionnaire t'aidera à enrichir ton **vocabulaire**.

Julie has a good vocabulary; she knows many words.
This dictionary will help increase your vocabulary.

3168   vocabulary

la voix

3169   voice

Le volcan crache de la lave.

3170   volcano

le volley-ball

3171   volleyball

volontaire, bénévole

3172   volunteer

Il a mangé quelque chose de mauvais; il **vomit**.

3173   to vomit

voter aux élections

3174   to vote

Un électeur vote.

3175   voter

la voyelle

A, E, I, O, U et Y sont **les seules voyelles** de l'alphabet.

A, E, I, O, U and Y are the only vowels in the alphabet.

3176   vowel

le voyage

3177   voyage

le vautour

3178   vulture

marcher dans l'eau, patauger

3179   to wade

la gaufre

3180   waffle

Le cheval tire **la charrette**.

3181   wagon/cart*

gémir, pleurer

3182   to wail

Lucie a **la taille** fine.

3183   waist

Carole **attend** l'autobus.

3184   to wait

réveiller

3185   to wake

Elle **marche** à grands pas.

3186   to walk

le mur

3187   wall

le portefeuille

3188   wallet

la noix

3189   walnut

le morse

3190   walrus

la baguette magique

3191   wand

se promener sans but, errer

3192   to wander

vouloir

Papa **veut** que Julie l'aide
à faire la vaisselle.
Elle **veut** bien l'**aider**, mais
il n'y a pas d'eau.

*Dad wants Julie to help him
wash the dishes.
She wants to help him but
there is no water.*

3193   to want

Julie a horreur de
la guerre.

3194   war

la garde-robe

3195   wardrobe

Cet **entrepôt** contient
beaucoup de marchandises.

3196   warehouse

un pull-over bien **chaud**

3197   warm

Viens te **réchauffer** près du feu!

3198   to warm up

avertir

3199   to warn

la garenne, la lapinière

3200   warren

Le guerrier part en guerre.

3201   warrior

la verrue

3202   wart

laver

3203   to wash up

la machine à laver, la laveuse

3204   washing machine

la salle de bains

3205   washroom/toilet*

Julie a été piquée par **une guêpe**.

3206   wasp

Il ne faut pas **gaspiller** la nourriture!

3207   to waste

la montre

3208   watch

Il **surveille** les poissons d'un œil attentif.

3209   to watch

l'eau

3210   water

un arrosoir

3211   watering can

Le cresson pousse au bord de l'eau.

3212   watercress

la chute d'eau

3213   waterfall

la pastèque

3214   watermelon

La botte est **imperméable**.

3215   waterproof

le ski nautique

3216   waterskiing

la vague

3217   wave

faire signe	Elle a les cheveux **ondulés**.	**La cire** de la bougie coule.	L'un est **faible**, l'autre est fort.
3218 to wave	3219 wavy	3220 wax	3221 weak
une arme dangereuse	Il **porte** des vêtements chauds.	**la belette**	Quel **temps** fait-il?
3222 weapon	3223 to wear	3224 weasel	3225 weather
tisser	un pied **palmé**	**le mariage**	le coin, le morceau triangulaire
3226 to weave	3227 web foot	3228 wedding	3229 wedge

mercredi

Mercredi est le jour de la semaine qui vient après mardi.
Le mercredi, Julie sort les poubelles.

Wednesday is the day after Tuesday.
On Wednesdays, Julie takes out the garbage.

3230 Wednesday

Le jardin est envahi par **les mauvaises herbes**.

3231 weed

La semaine a sept jours.

3232 week

la fin de semaine, le week-end

La fin de semaine est faite du samedi et du dimanche. Tante Lucie nous rendra visite ce **week-end**.

Saturday and Sunday make a weekend.
Aunt Lucie will visit us this weekend.

3233 weekend

Il **pleure** parce qu'il est triste.	**peser**	Ce dessin est **étrange, bizarre**.	Hélène **souhaite la bienvenue** à son ami.
3234 to weep	3235 to weigh	3236 weird	3237 to welcome

Ne tombe pas dans **le puits!**

3238   well

Je me sens bien.

3239   I feel **well.**

L'ouest est opposé à l'est.

3240   west

humide, mouillé

3241   wet

la baleine

3243   whale

le quai

3244   wharf

quoi, que

Quoi? **Que** dis-tu?
Que veux-tu pour le petit déjeuner?

*What? What did you say?
What do you want for breakfast?*

3245   what

mouiller

3242   to wet

Le blé donne de la farine.

3246   wheat

la roue

3247   wheel

la brouette

3248   wheelbarrow

la chaise roulante

3249   wheelchair

quand

Quand tante Émilie viendra-t-elle nous voir?
Quand elle aura ses vacances.

*When is Aunt Émilie coming to see us?
When she takes her holidays.*

3250   when

où

Nous sommes perdus et maman n'a pas la moindre idée **où** nous sommes.
Je sais **où** c'est, mais je n'arrive pas à le retrouver.

*We are lost and Mother has no idea where we are.
I know where it is, but I cannot find it.*

3251   where

Il ne sait pas **lequel** choisir.

3252   which one

pleurnicher

3253   to whine

le fouet

3254   whip

un engoulevent

3255   whippoorwill

Le fouet sert à battre les œufs et la crème.

3256   whisk

la moustache du chat

3257   whisker

Qu'est-ce qu'elle lui **chuchote** à l'oreille? 3258 to whisper	**le sifflet** 3259 whistle	**siffler** 3260 to whistle	**blanc** 3261 white
Qui y va? 3262 Who is going?	**pourquoi** Je veux savoir **pourquoi** Julie a pris ma cravate. **Pourquoi** ne peut-elle pas s'en souvenir? *I want to know why Julie took my tie.* *Why can she not remember?* 3263 why	**La mèche** brûle lentement. 3264 wick	**mauvais, méchant** 3265 wicked
large 3266 wide	Madame Arthaud est **la femme** de Monsieur Arthaud. 3267 wife	Le lion est un animal **sauvage**. 3268 The lion is a wild animal.	**Le saule** a de longues branches. 3269 willow
Les fleurs **se fanent** quand elles manquent d'eau. 3270 to wilt	**rusé, astucieux** 3271 wily	**gagner** 3272 to win	**grimacer de douleur** 3273 to wince
Le vent souffle avec rage. 3274 wind	**remonter** 3275 to wind	**le blouson, le coupe-vent** 3276 windbreaker	**Le moulin à vent** a des ailes. 3277 windmill

la fenêtre

3278 window

le pare-brise

3279 windshield/windscreen*

Le vin est réservé aux adultes.

3280 wine

une aile

3281 wing

cligner de l'œil

3282 to wink

Est-ce que tu aimes **l'hiver**?

3283 winter

Essuie bien, s'il te plaît.

3284 to wipe

Les oiseaux sont perchés sur **le fil**.

3285 wire

sage, prudent

Grand-père est un vieil homme **sage**.
Julie, crois-tu qu'il est **prudent** de te promener seule en forêt?

Grandfather is a wise old man.
Julie, do you think it is wise to walk in the forest alone?

3286 wise

faire **un vœu**

3287 to make a wish

la sorcière

3288 witch

le magicien

3289 wizard

le loup

3290 wolf

la femme

3291 woman

se demander

3292 to wonder

un **merveilleux** feu d'artifice

3293 wonderful

le bois

3294 wood

Le pivert pique le tronc de l'arbre.

3295 woodpecker

Ils se promènent dans **les bois**.

3296 woods

le travail du bois

3297 woodwork

Elle tricote avec
de **la laine**.

3298   wool

Quel drôle de **mot**!

GLÜRP

3299   word

le travail

3300   work

Elle **travaille** au jardin.

3301   to work

un atelier

3303   workshop

le monde

3304   world

Le ver se tortille.

3305   worm

faire des exercices physiques

3302   to work out

s'inquiéter

3306   to worry

la blessure

3307   wound

emballer, envelopper

3308   to wrap

la guirlande, la couronne
de fleurs

3309   wreath

une épave

3310   wreck

le roitelet

3311   wren

Ils **luttent** férocement.

3312   to wrestle

tordre le linge

3313   to wring

le poignet

3314   wrist

la montre-bracelet

3315   wristwatch

écrire

3316   to write

mal, mauvais

C'est **mal** de tricher
et de voler.
Je pense que notre autobus
va dans le **mauvais** sens.

*It is wrong to cheat and
to lie.
I think our bus is going the
wrong way.*

3317   wrong

les rayons X, la radiographie

3318   X-ray

le xylophone

3319   xylophone

le yacht

3320   yacht

la cour

3321   yard/garden*

Est-ce qu'il **bâille** d'ennui ou de sommeil?

3322   to yawn

un an, une année

3323   year

hurler, crier

3324   to yell

jaune

3325   yellow

oui

C'est **oui**, c'est non, ou c'est peut-être? Si tu dis **oui**, tu dois être sûr.

Is it yes, is it no, or is it maybe? If you say yes, you had better be sure.

3326   yes

hier

Hier, Julie a été malade parce qu'elle avait mangé trop de crème glacée. Qu'est-ce que tu as fait **hier**?

Yesterday, Julie was sick from eating too much ice cream. What did you do yesterday?

3327   yesterday

Isabelle doit **céder** le passage.

3328   to yield/give way*

le jaune d'œuf

3329   yolk

jeune et vieux

3330   young

le zèbre qu'a dessiné Julie

3331   zebra

zéro

3332   zero

la fermeture éclair

3333   zipper/zip*

le zoo

3334   zoo

filer à toute allure

3335   to zoom

La courgette est le dernier mot de Julie.

3336   zucchini/courgette*

a

à 117
à longs poils 1091
à part 78
à réaction 1485, 1486
abaisser 1699
abandonner 839
abattre (s') 2898
abeille (une) 216
abîmé 724
aboyer 174
abri (un) 2596
abricot (un) 87
absent 4
accélérateur (un) 5
accélérer 2747
accent (un) 6
accident (un) 7
accidenté 2470
accordéon (un) 8
accorder 1184
accrocher 1261
accroupir (s') 2780
accumuler 1341
accuser 9
acheter 398
acide (un) 12, 2734
acier (un) 2807
acrobate (un, une) 14
additionner 16
adieu 956
adorer 19
adresse (une) 17
adroit 1258
adulte (un, une) 20, 1221
aéroglisseur (un) 1390
aéroport (un) 40
affaire (une) 1750
affamé 2352
affiche (une) 2211
affiloir (un) 2585
affreux 136
affûteuse (une) 2586
Afrique 25
âge (un) 30
agenouiller (s') 1541
agent de police (un)
    615, 2185
agente de police (une)
    2186

agile 31
agneau (un) 1561
agréable 2157
agriculteur (un) 958
agripper 1207
aider 1308
aigle (un) 858
aiglefin (un) 1235
aiguille (une) 1890
aiguisé 2584
ail (un) 1107
aile (une) 3281
aile d'auto (une) 976
ailleurs (d') 239
aimable 1176
aimant (un) 1713
aimer 1644, 1695, 1696
air (un) 36
aire de jeux (une) 2155
airelle (une) 1394
aisselle (une) 98
album de photos (un)
    43
algue (une) 2553
alimenter 972
allée (une) 41
alléger 1640
aller 1157
alligator (un) 48
allongé 1930
allumer 1638, 2897,
    3102
allumette (une) 1748
alouette (une) 1577,
    2670
alphabet (un) 54
aluminium (un) 58
amande (une) 49
amasser 1341
ambulance (une) 60
amende (une) 991
amer 258
ami (un) 1073
amiral (un) 18
ampoule (une) 278,
    1639
amusant 1089
amuser (s') 1085
amygdale (une) 3022
an (un) 3323
ananas (un) 2126

ancien 63
ancre (une) 62
âne (un) 803
ange de mer (un) 1826
angle (un) 64
anguille (une) 875
animal (un) 66
animal familier (un)
    2092
animer 1668
année (une) 3323
anniversaire (un) 254
annoncer 68
annuler 410
Antarctique (l') 72
antilope (une) 73
août 126
apercevoir (s') 2361
aplatir 1020
apparaître 82
appareil-photo (un) 414
appartenir 231
appât (un) 148
appeler 409
applaudir 83, 537
apporter 351
apprécier 898
apprendre 1602
apprivoisé 2923
approcher 86
appui-tête (un) 1289
appuyer 2233, 2261
après 26
après-midi (un, une)
    27
aquarium (un) 90
arachide (une) 2060
araignée (une) 2752
arbitre (un) 2382
arbre (un) 3065
arbre à feuilles
    persistantes (un) 913
arbuste (un) 391, 2630
arc (un) 322
arc-en-ciel (un) 2338
arche (une) 91
architecte (un, une) 92
Arctique (l') 93
ardoise (une) 2676
arête (une) 2420
argent (l') 1824, 2644

argent liquide (l') 454
argile (une) 540
arme (une) 3222
armé de piquants 2238
armoire (une) 401
armure (une) 97
arracher 2948
arranger 100
arrêt (un) 2829
arrêt d'autobus (un)
    390
arrêter 101, 2830
arrêter un instant (s')
    2050
arrière 1335
arriver 102, 1265
arrosoir (un) 3211
artichaut (un) 104
articulation (une) 1494,
    1548
artiste (un, une) 105
as (un) 10
ascenseur (un) 886
Asie (l') 109
asperge (une) 112
aspirine (une) 113
assassiner 1858
assez 900
assiette (une) 2151
assoiffer (être) 2977
asticot (un) 1710
astronaute (un, une)
    115
astronome (un, une)
    116
astucieux 3271
atelier (un) 3303
athlète (un, une) 118
atlas (un) 119
atmosphère (une) 120
atome (un) 121
âtre (un) 1002
attacher 122, 250, 960,
    2997
attaque (une) 2334
attaquer à (s') 2906
atteindre 2357
attendre 924, 3184
attendre à (s') 924
attention (faire) 123

m

moquer 1815
morceau (le) 2110
morceau de charbon
(le) 529
morceau triangulaire
(le) 3229
mordre 256
morse (le) 3190
morsure (la) 257
mort 736
mortel 962
mortier (le) 1835
morue (la) 570
mosaïque (la) 1836
mot (le) 3299
moteur (le) 896, 1840
motocyclette (la) 1841
motte (la) 1843
mouche (la) 1036
mouchoir (le) 1264
moudre 1206
mouette (la) 1230,
2545
moufle (la) 1811
mouillé 725, 3241
mouiller 3242
moule (la) 1864
moule (le) 1842
moulin (le) 1794
moulin à vent (le) 3277
moulinet (le) 2381
mourir 763
mourir de faim 2799
mousse (la) 1039, 1838
mousse de savon (la)
1583
moustache (la) 1847,
3257
moustiquaire (la) 2538
moustique (le) 1837
moutarde (la) 1866
mouton (le) 2592
mouvement (le) 1850
moyen 1766
mule (la) 1855
multiplier 1856
mur (le) 3187
mûr 2431
mûre (la) 260
muscle (le) 1859
museau (le) 1867

musée (le) 1860
muselière (la) 1867
musicienne (la) 1863
musique (la) 1862
myrtille (la) 292

n

nageoire (la) 990
nager 2893
nain (le) 856, 1790
naissance (la) 253
naître 312
nappe (la) 2903
nation (la) 1873
nature (la) 1878
naturel 1877
naufrage (le) 2605
nauséabond 2702
navet (le) 3105
naviguer 1880
navire (le) 2604
navire-citerne (le) 2928
ne pas 75
ne rien 426
nécessaire 1883
nectar (le) 1886
nectarine (la) 1887
négliger 1891
neige (la) 2712
neige à demi-fondue
(la) 2696
neige fondante (la)
2681
nerf (le) 1897
nerveux 1898
net 1882
nettoyeur à sec (le)
844
neuf, neuve 1902
neuf 1914
neuvième (le, la) 1915
neveu (le) 1896
nez (le) 1923
ni l'un ni l'autre 1894
niche (la) 1514
nickel (le) 1908
nid (le) 1899
nièce (la) 1910

niveau (le) 1625
noble 1917
noeud (le) 1546
noeud papillon (le) 323
noir 259
noir (le) 730
noisetier (le) 1285
noisette (la) 1286
noix (la) 1924, 3189
noix d'acajou (la) 455
noix de coco (la) 569
nom (le) 1873
nom de famille (le)
2879
nombril (le) 230
non 1916
nord (le) 1922
note (la) 1738
nouer 2997
nouilles (les) 2040
nourrir 972
nourrisson (le) 1435
nourriture (la) 1043
nouveau 28
nouvelle (la) 1903
nu 171, 1872
nuage (le) 553
nuit (la) 1911
nulle part 77
nylon (le) 1926

o

oasis (une) 1929
oblong 1930
observer 1931
occuper 392
océan (un) 1932
octobre 1934
octogone (un) 1933
odeur (une) 1937
odomètre (un) 1936
oeil (un) 932
oeillet (un) 443
oeillet d'Inde (un) 1736
oeuf (un) 876
officier (un) 1940
offrir 1939
oie (une) 1169

oignon (un) 1950
oiseau (un) 252
oiseau moqueur (un)
1816
oiseau-mouche (un)
1398
oisif 1421
olive (une) 1945
ombre (une) 2577
omelette (une) 1946
once (une) 1970
oncle (un) 3123
ondulation (une) 2432
ondulé 3219
ongle (un) 1869
opération (une) 1954
opossum (un) 1955
or (l') 1164
orage (un) 2834, 2990
orange 1959
orange (une) 1958
orchestre (un) 162,
1961
orchidée (une) 1962
ordinateur (un) 601
ordures (les) 1103
oreille (une) 859
oreiller (un) 2119
oreillons (les) 1857
orge (une) 176
orgue (un) 1965
origan (l') 1964
orignal (un) 1833
orme (un) 888
ornière (une) 2481
orphelin (un) 1967
orteil (un) 3013
ortie (une) 1900
os (un) 303
oseille (l') 2730
ou 1957
où 3251
oublier 1052
ouest (l') 3240
oui 3326
ouïe (une) 1139
ouragan (un) 1404
ourlet (un) 1310
ours (un) 205
ourson (un) 691
outil (un) 3023

rosée (la) 756
rossignol (le) 1912
rôti (le) 2439
roue (la) 3247
roue de secours (la) 2741
rouge 2377
rouge à lèvres (le) 1660
rouge-gorge (le) 2441
rougeole (la) 1760
rougir 294
rouille (la) 2480
rouleau (le) 2447
rouleau à pâtisserie (le) 2450
rouler 2448
roussir 2531
route (la) 2437
royal 2464
ruban (le) 2415
ruban adhésif (le) 2930
rubis (le) 2467
ruche (la) 80, 218, 1340
rude 564
rue (la) 2847
ruelle (la) 47
rugir 2438
rugueux 2460
ruine (la) 2471
ruisseau (le) 356, 667
rusé 3271

S

s'il vous plaît 2158
sable (le) 2498
sables mouvants (les) 2315
sablier (le) 1388
sabot (le) 1365
sabrer 2675
sac (le) 147, 2215, 2294, 2483
sac de couchage (le) 2679
sacoche (la) 2294
sacré 2484

sacrer 1354
sage 3286
saigner 274
sain 1291
saisir 559, 1207, 2560
saison (la) 2550
salade (la) 2492
sale 776, 989, 1204
saleté (la) 775
salir 2700
salle à manger (la) 771
salle de bains (la) 193, 3205
salon (le) 1669
saluer 1201, 2496
salut 1305
samedi (le) 2505
sandale (la) 2499
sandwich (le) 2500
sang (le) 284
sanglier (le) 295
sans espoir 1370
sapin (le) 996, 2125, 2777
sardine (la) 2502
satellite (le) 2503
satin (le) 2504
sauce (la) 2506
saucisse (la) 2507
saule (le) 3269
saumon (le) 2494
saupoudrer 2775
sauter 1368, 1500, 2216, 2665
sauter (faire) 270
sauter dans 1501
sauter sur 1502
sauterelle (la) 1189, 1679
sauteur (le) 1503
sautiller 1368
sauvage 3268
sauver 2404
sauver (se) 2476
savoir 1547
savoir parfaitement faire 1746
savon (le) 2715
savourer 898
savoureux 2939
scarabée (le) 221

scène (la) 2523
scène du théâtre (la) 2786
scie (la) 2509
scier 2510
scintiller 3115
sciure (la) 2511
scooter (le) 2530
scout (le) 2533
sculpteur (le) 2542
seau (le) 368, 1994
sec 842
sèche-cheveux (le) 1240
sécher 843
sécheuse (la) 845
second (le) 2554
secouer 2579
secourir 2404
secours (le) 34
secret (le) 2555
seigle (le) 2482
sel (le) 2495
selle (la) 2486
semaine (la) 3232
sembler 2559
semer 2737
sensible 2565
sentier (le) 2046
sentinelle (la) 2567
sentir 2701
sentir (se) 973
sentir mauvais 2380
sentir très mauvais 2821
séparé 78
sept 2570
septembre 2568
septième (le, la) 2571
serpent (le) 2707
serpent à sonnettes (le) 2350
serpentin (le) 573
serre (la) 1200
serrer 536, 2781, 2999
serrer dans ses bras 890
serrer les uns contre les autres (se) 1395
serrure (la) 1677
service (le) 966

serviette (la) 349, 1874, 3039
servir 2569
seuil (le) 2983
seul 51, 1951
seul (être) 1684
sève (la) 2501
shampooing (le) 2581
short (le) 2618
si 1422
siècle (le) 476
siège (le) 2551
siffler 3260
sifflet (le) 3259
signaler 2639
signature (la) 2640
silencieux 2641
simple 2645
singe (le) 79, 1825
singulier (le) 2647
sirène (la) 1774, 2651
sirop (le) 2901
siroter 2650
six 2654
sixième (le, la) 2655
ski (le) 2661
ski nautique (le) 3216
skier 2662
soeur (la) 2652
sofa (le) 2719
soigné 299
soigneux 2995
soirée (la) 2033
sol (le) 1029, 1216
soldat (le) 2721
soldes (les) 172, 2493
sole (la) 2722
soleil (le) 2868
solitaire 1684
sombre 768
sommeil (avoir) 840
sommeiller 810
sommet (le) 2058, 3028
somnolent (se sentir) 2680
son de la cloche (le) 2059
sonner 2426
sorcier (le) 2728

sorcière (la) 3288
sorte (la) 1528
sortie de secours (la) 999
sortir 922, 2814, 2916
souche (la) 2859
souci (le) 1736
soudain 2863
souffler 290
souffrant 1425
souhaiter la bienvenue 3237
soulever 1297, 1636, 2103, 2340
soulier (le) 2609
soupe (la) 2733
souper (le) 2875
soupirer 2637
source (la) 2774
sourcil (le) 359, 933
sourd 737
souris (la) 1846
sous 3124
sous-marin (le) 2860
sous-sol (le) 186
sous-vêtement (le) 3126
soustraire 2861
soutenir 2261
soutien-gorge (le) 328
souvenir (se) 2368, 2395
souvent 1941
souverain (le) 2473
spectacle (le) 2085
sphère (la) 2750
spirale (la) 2758
sprinter 2776
squelette (le) 2659
station-service (la) 1113, 2800
stationner 2025
statue (la) 2802
steak (le) 2804
stop (le) 2829
stupide 2643
stylo (le) 2074
succulent 2939
sucer 2862
sucette (la) 1683
sucré 2891

sucre (le) 2864
sud (le) 2735
suivre 1042
superbe 1196
supermarché (le) 2874
supplier 2159
sur 1947
sûr 610, 2876
surface (la) 2877
surnom (le) 1909
surprise-partie (la) 2880
surveiller 3209
suspendre 1259
sycomore (le) 2900

t

table (la) 2902
tableau (le) 2108
tableau de bord (le) 732
tableau noir (le) 262
tablier (le) 89
tabouret (le) 2827
tache (la) 2767, 2787
tâche (la) 2937
tache de rousseur (la) 1067
taie d'oreiller (la) 2120
taillader 2675
taille (la) 2656, 3183
taille-crayons (le) 2587
tailler 546, 2271
tailleur (le) 2909
talent (le) 2919
talon (le) 1302
tambour (le) 841
tambourin (le) 2922
tante (la) 127
tapage (le) 2328
taper 2218
tapis (le) 446
tarte (la) 2109, 2936
tartelette (la) 2936
tas (le) 1292, 2116
tasse (la) 696
taupe (la) 1820
taureau (le) 375

taxi (le) 2940
télégramme (le) 2949
téléphone (le) 2099, 2950
téléphone public (le) 2272
téléphoner 411, 2951
télescope (le) 2952
télévision (la) 2953
température (la) 2956
tempête (la) 2834
tempête de neige (la) 279
temps (le) 3225
tenaille (la) 2161
tenir 1348
tenir debout (se) 2794
tenir voûté (se) 2694
tennis (le) 2958, 2959
tente (la) 2960
tenue (la) 1972
tenue élégante (la) 953
tenue habillée (la) 953
terminal (le) 2962
terre (la) 863, 1216, 1566
têtard (le) 2907
tête (la) 1287
thé (le) 2941
théâtre (le) 2966
théière (la) 2945
thermomètre (le) 2968
thym (le) 2992
tiède 1702
tige (la) 2811
tigre (le) 2998
timbre (le) 2793
timide 2633
tire-bouchon (le) 628
tirer 1279, 2277, 2612, 3095
tiroir (le) 818
tisser 3226
tissu (le) 550
toast (le) 3010
toboggan (le) 2683
toile d'araignée (la) 567
toilettes (les) 3015
toison (la) 1024
toit (le) 2451
tomate (la) 3016

tombe (la) 3017
tomber 946, 3030, 3097
tomber avec fracas 659
tomber dans les pommes 2035
tomber en panne 940
tomber par terre 947
tondeuse à gazon (la) 1593
tondre 1852
tonne (la) 3021
tonneau (le) 179
tonnerre (le) 2989
tordre 236, 3117, 3313
tordu 675
tornade (la) 3032
torrent (le) 3033
tortiller 3117
tortue (la) 3034, 3109
toucher 3036
toujours 59
toupie (la) 3029
tour (la) 3040
tour (le) 3070
tourbe (la) 1191, 2064
tourelle (la) 3108
tournant (le) 235
tourne-disque (le) 2374, 3106
tourner 2755, 3100, 3103, 3104, 3116
tournesol (le) 2871
tournevis (le) 2540
tournoyer 3116
tous 46
tous deux 315
tousser 638
tracer 3043
tracteur (le) 3045
train (le) 3051
traîner 812
trait d'union (le) 1412
tramway (le) 3077
tranchant 2584
tranchée (la) 3067
trancher 709
tranquille 2316
transparent 3056
transpirer 2888

transporter 1279, 3057
trapèze (le) 3060
travail (le) 1490, 2937, 3300
travail du bois (le) 3297
travailler 3301
travers (à) 15
traverser 679
traversier (le) 978
trébucher 3076
trèfle (le) 554
tremblement de terre (le) 864
trembler 2322, 3066
tremplin (le) 3055
très 3151
trésor (le) 3064
triangle (le) 3069
tricher 498
tricot (le) 2889
tricoter 1543
tricycle (le) 3072
trier 2732
triste 2485, 3128
trognon de pomme (le) 85
trois 2982
troisième (le, la) 2976
trompe (la) 3088
trompette (la) 3085
tronc (le) 3087
tronçonneuse (la) 481
trône (le) 2985
trop 1853
troquer 2886
trotter 3078
trottoir (le) 2636
trou (le) 1350
troupeau (le) 1315
truc (le) 3070
truelle (la) 3082
truie (la) 2736
truite (la) 3081
tube (le) 2711, 3093
tuer 1523
tulipe (la) 3096
tunnel (le) 3098
turquoise 3107
tuyau (le) 1381

u

un, une 1949
unie 2139
uniforme (un) 3130
unir 1656
université (une) 3131
urgence (une) 892
usé 2575
usine (une) 938
utile 3139
utiliser 3137
utiliser (tout) 3138

V

vacances (les) 1351, 3140
vacarme (le) 2328
vache (la) 650
vagabond (le) 3053
vague (la) 3217
vairon (le) 1799
vaisseau spatial (le) 2738
vaisselle (la) 516, 784
valise (la) 2866
vanter (se) 297, 330
vapeur (la) 2806, 3141
vaporiser 2770
varicelle (la) 509
vase (le) 3143
vautour (le) 3178
veau (le) 408, 3144
véhicule (le) 3146
veine (la) 3148
vélo (le) 244, 246
vendre 2562
vendredi (le) 1071
vénéneux 2181
venimeux 2181
venin (le) 3149
venir 587
vent (le) 3274
ventilateur (le) 952
ver (le) 3305
verger (le) 1960
vérifier 499
véritable 3084
vérité (la) 3090

vernir 3142
verre (le) 1150, 1151
verre de lunettes (le) 1616
verrouiller 1676
verrue (la) 2122, 3202
vers 99
verser 2219
vert 1198
veste (la) 1473
vestibule (le) 1242
veston (le) 272
vêtement (le) 551
vétérinaire (le, la) 3153
viande (la) 1762
victime (la) 3154
vide 893
vide (le) 1101
vie (la) 1634
vierge 267
vieux 1944
vigne (la) 3160
village (le) 3158
ville (la) 534, 3041
vin (le) 3280
vinaigre (le) 3161
violet 2292
violette (la) 3162
violon (le) 3163
virgule (la) 591
vis (la) 2539
visa (le) 3164
visage (le) 937
viser 35
visible 3165
visière (la) 3167
visiter 3166
visqueux 2685
vitrine (la) 2615
vivant 45
vivre 1667
vocabulaire (le) 3168
voeu (le) 3287
voie (la) 1570, 3044
voie ferrée (la) 2336
voile (la) 2488
voile (le) 3147
voilette (la) 3147
voilier (le) 2490
voir 2556
voisin (le) 1893

voiture (la) 436
voiture d'enfant (la) 141, 447
voiture de pompiers (la) 998
voix (la) 3169
voix enrouée (la) 1342
voix rauque (la) 1342
vol (le) 1027
volcan (le) 3170
voler 1038, 2805
volet (le) 2632
voleur (le) 2440, 2970
volley-ball (le) 3171
volontaire (le, la) 3172
vomir 2987, 3173
voter 3174
vouloir 3193
voyage (le) 3075, 3177
voyager 3061
voyelle (la) 3176
vrai 1122, 2360, 3084
vraiment 2362
vraisemblable 1645
vue (la) 3157

W

week-end (le) 3233

X

xylophone (le) 3319

y

yacht (le) 3320
youyou (le) 770

Z

zèbre (le) 3331
zéro (le) 3332
zona (le) 2602
zoo (le) 3334